High Praises for R

"*Road to Waubeek* reveals fascinatir

his connections to Marvin Cone, Paul Engle, and Grant Wood. Feller's research adds another layer to the artistic and literary legacies these men cultivated in eastern Iowa."
—Ranelle Knight-Lueth, PhD, Assistant Professor of Art History, Director of Galleries and Collections, Coe College

"I found *Road To Waubeek* by author and good friend Barb Feller to be a wonderful and satisfying account of the timeless beauty and value of Linn County, Iowa. There is so much to discover and appreciate, including the richness of the friendships between Jay Sigmund, Grant Wood, and Paul Engle. These pages help capture the essence of an incredibly creative and meaningful time in the Midwestern Heartland. A joy to read!"
—Mark Stoffer Hunter, Historian, Linn County Historical Society (The History Center)

"A wonderful tribute to the 'Poet of the Wapsipinicon Valley.' Jay Sigmund's Regionalist influence can be seen in the work of contemporaries Grant Wood and Paul Engle. Jay's advice to Wood: Stay home and paint what you know best,' led to Cedar Rapids becoming the 'prairie art capital.' A review in the *Cedar Rapids Gazette* of Grant Wood's *Woman with Plants,* stated, 'Wood is now doing with pigments what Jay Sigmund is doing with words.' Sigmund's work and influence on fellow artists harkens us back to a time of reassuring words and images of the American Heartland during the Great Depression. Barbara Feller's profile of Jay Sigmund's life and his significant influence on the modern Regionalist movement are shared with an appreciation of how this author's personality helped define the character of the people of Iowa."
—Jim Jacobmeyer, Founder and President, The Artisan's Sanctuary, Marion, Iowa

"Who knew a man born in the tiny town of Waubeek, Iowa, would be in the right place at the right time to influence the 20th Century's most important artists and art movements? Without Jay Sigmund, Grant Wood might have toiled in obscurity, imitating French Impressionists instead of creating American Regionalism. Without Jay Sigmund, Paul Engle might have owned a grocery store, instead of making the University of Iowa Writers' Workshop renown throughout the world. Peeling back the layers of this fascinating man, Barb Feller invites us to join her on a unique journey, one that demonstrates how a single life can not only have a lasting impact on a community, but on the art and culture of an entire generation."

—Dennis Green, Arts & Culture Editor & General Manager KCCK FM, author, *Traveler*

"*Road to Waubeek*, is a historical gem. Demonstrating how great artists are nurtured by individuals in a community who recognize their specialness, encourage them and validate their early thinking and works. Feller has discovered just such a person, Jay G. Sigmund, a Cedar Rapids insurance agent, who was once a well-known Midwestern author, but even more significant, he became a friend and inspiration to two of Iowa's most important sons: artist Grant Wood and poet/parent of the University of Iowa's Writers' Workshop, Paul Engle. Feller delineates the importance of Sigmund's friendship with these two, and also documents his importance and support for the development of Cedar Rapids' Community Theater and the Art Center's beginning collection. This slim volume is important for its insight into Iowa history, Middle West artistic culture, and the literary history of American poetry. Even more important, her book demonstrates the power of friendship."

—Ann Struthers, author of two new poetry chapbooks, *Aleppo Burning* and *The Kindness of Crocodiles*

"Ms. Feller approaches her subject as a mystery. She finds a mysterious archival box which tempts her into a universe of unanswered questions. The book is written just this way. The author enters a world of civilization, discipline, and inspiration inside an unlikely place. The book tempts the reader with revelation after revelation, painting vivid pictures. You want to follow the trail which connects familiar names in the high reaches of poetry and art to the personality and genius of one Jay G. Sigmund, a true Iowan poet, whose importance may have been lost if it were not for Ms Feller's scholarship. Barbara Feller reaches into the style of a more formal and serious time in her writing, and the result is engaging. The book brings a lost time and place to life. Declaring the significance of this community of small places as pivotal in the evolution of American letters and art."
—Don Schaeffer, PhD, author, *Banzai & Four Stories and Their Poems*

"Coming from Missouri and living in Iowa for nearly forty years I had heard the name of Mr. Sigmund but did not know his true significance to Eastern Iowa and the world of art and literature. Barb Feller has found the pieces of a far flung puzzle and did the work for us in putting the picture all together for we of following generations. *Road to Waubeek* is a grand story about a grand fellow."
—Cary J. Hahn, Classic KMRY Radio News Director, Former CBS 2 Iowa Traveler

Road to Waubeek

Discovering Jay G. Sigmund

Barbara Feller

Carolyn,
Hope you enjoy travels along the Road to Waubeek.
Barbara Feller
Oct. 16, 2018

Ice Cube Press, LLC
North Liberty, Iowa, USA

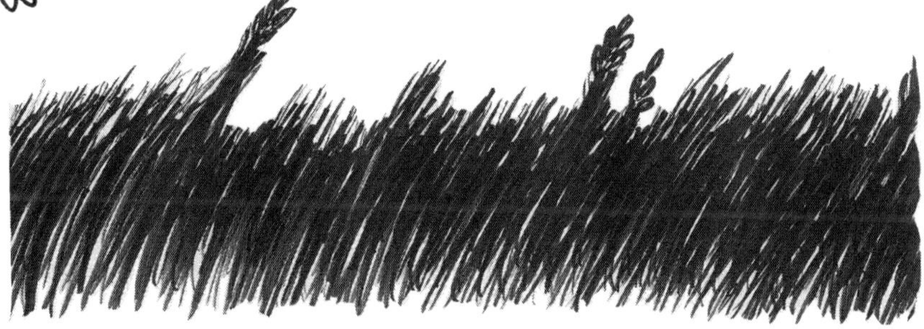

Road To Waubeek: Discovering Jay G. Sigmund

ISBN 9781948509008

Library of Congress Cataloging Number: 2018933995

Ice Cube Press, LLC (Est. 1991)
North Liberty, Iowa 52317
steve@icecubepress.com
www.icecubepress.com

The paper used in this publication meets the minimum requirements of the American National Standard for Information Sciences—Permanence of Paper for Printed Library Materials, ANSI Z39.48-1992.

Design & Editorial Assistance, as well as the Grass Drawing used throughout by Erin McInerney.

Thanks to the Cone family for permission to use the cover image:
Marvin Cone
Road to Waubeek
oil on canvas
1940-41
Gift of Dr. Irving Churchill
Coe College Permanent Art Collection
Photo by Mark Tade, 2006

Credits: All photos, unless noted, are provided by Barbara Feller and Virginia Sigmund Meyers' collection. Author photo: Tessa Leone Photography and Design Co. Additional credits provided at end of book.

This book is dedicated in memory of:
Jane Cooper and Virginia Sigmund Meyers.

"He wanted not an ivory tower but simply
the water tower of his own village."
—Paul Engle, (Nov. 8, 1939),
describing Jay Sigmund

Jay G. Sigmund

The name we called him, and the face,
They go, when a man dies,
But he has left in the troubled air
The honesty of quiet eyes.

Here was a man who equally
Could love and understand
The nourishing rain of heaven,
And the sweat of a working hand.

He knew the fields where mushrooms grow,
Where a boy could find, with luck,
Indian arrowheads, and the wild
Cry of the autumn duck.

He knew where the last old mill wheel turned,
White bones in the buffalo wallow,
Hidden rattlesnake dens and cliffs
With deep nests of the swallow.

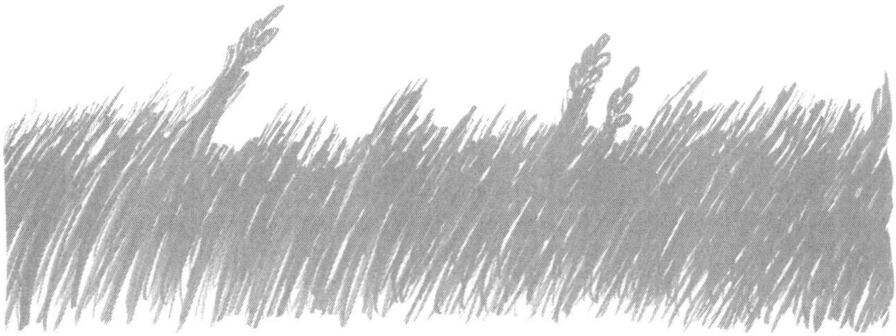

His were friendly country ways
That grew from prairie loam
Like native corn; he took men in
To his open hands and his home.

The rivers of Iowa have heard
His low voice talking,
The hills of Iowa have borne
The weight of his walking.

We knew him too, we were his friends
From the farming country around
The Wapisi land where he lived and worked,
We know the feel of that ground.

We will die different men because
We knew him face to face.
Let us bury him now with his weather and crops,
And say—He belongs to this place.

—Paul Engle

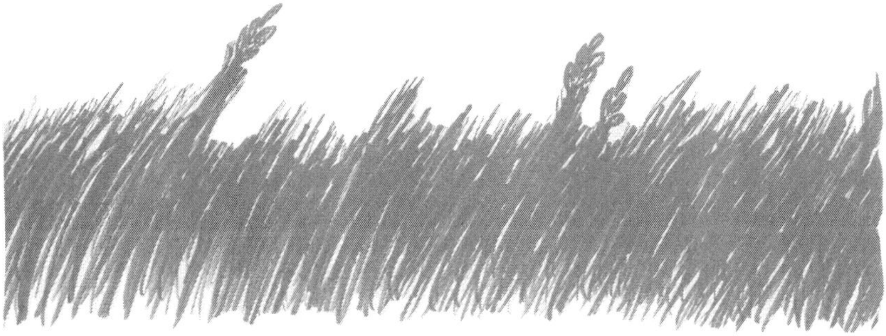

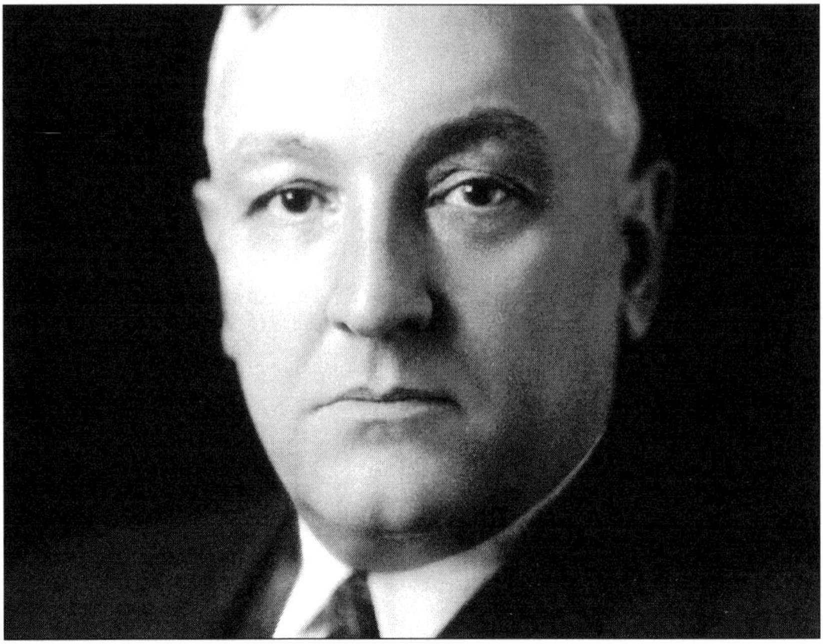

Jay Sigmund, 1928

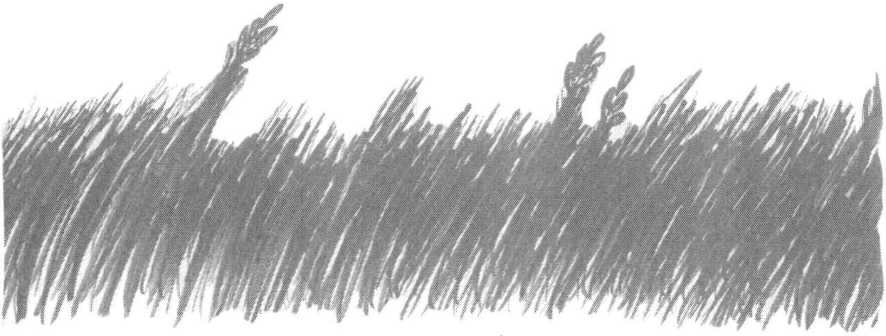

INTRODUCTION

In 2001, when I was first hired as an educator at the Linn County History Center in downtown Cedar Rapids, my desk was inside the archival library. I enjoyed being surrounded by books and papers from Iowa's past and will admit they made me feel very special in turn. After all, if someone wanted to meet with me they had to be let into a climate controlled room by someone who knew the security code. This seemed to mean I was as special as the history that surrounded me.

Being a native New Yorker, however, I was no expert on Iowa. So, when I was asked to design a class for upper elementary grade students on the values and importance of archives, my environment served as the catalyst for how I would go about this task.

As luck would have it, I came across an archival box which contained a booklet of poetry, some photos, and a letter typed by Jay G. Sigmund in response to an apparent fan of his. These items were perfect for my task. Among other things, Sigmund's letter, to a Dr. Stookey, described his place of birth "a mile south of the village of Waubeek," locations his family lived over the years, and named Rabbit Grove as a one-room school he attended. The booklet, simply entitled *Cedar Rapids,* was a poetic tracing of that city's history.

I knew the museum archives included colorful nineteenth century Linn County plat maps (see below) which detail rural property outlines of waterways, land parcels over five acres, and names of the landowners. I figured students would enjoy using these colorfully illustrated atlases while following Sigmund's early journey. Furthermore, The History Center was building an exhibit on country schools in Linn County and had asked my fellow historian, Mark Hunter, to develop an accompanying tour.

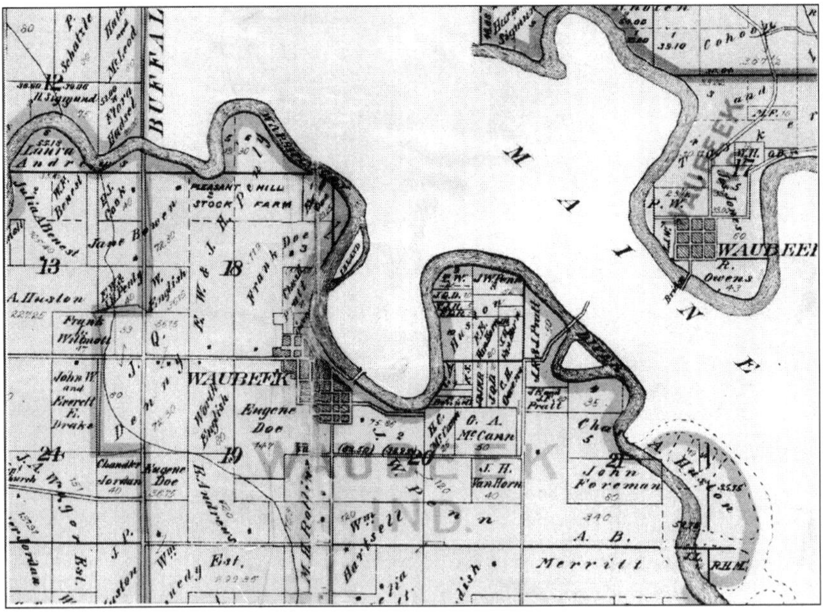

Plat Map, Linn County, Linn Co. History Center

Thinking we might be able to locate Rabbit Grove school, Mark invited me to come along during his explorations. I knew this type of journey was exactly what was needed to help me usher my future students toward a living past.

There was only one problem: I had no idea who Jay G. Sigmund was! Why was his letter written on Cedar Rapids Life Insurance Company stationery? How did the letter rate enough importance to be saved in an archive? And how did Mr. Sigmund come to write a lengthy poem on the history of Cedar Rapids?

Tracing the answers to these questions led me to discover an insurance salesman who had inspired the leading artists and authors of his time and inspired me as well. Now, a full fifteen years after this introduction to Mr. Sigmund, the walls of my house are lined with prints of art inspired by Jay G. Sigmund and my book shelves include a vast collection of his works.

These last years I've delved into the archives of the Central City Historical Society, the Cedar Rapids Public Library, the Special Collections at the University of Iowa Library, and even found first hand descriptions of Jay Sigmund's home in the main branch of the New York City Public Library. In addition to all this, I am proud to be accepted as a good friend to several surviving members of his family.

I am excited to share my discoveries with you in the hopes that you will enjoy learning about Jay G. Sigmund as much as I have.

Happy reading!
Barbara Feller, January, 2018

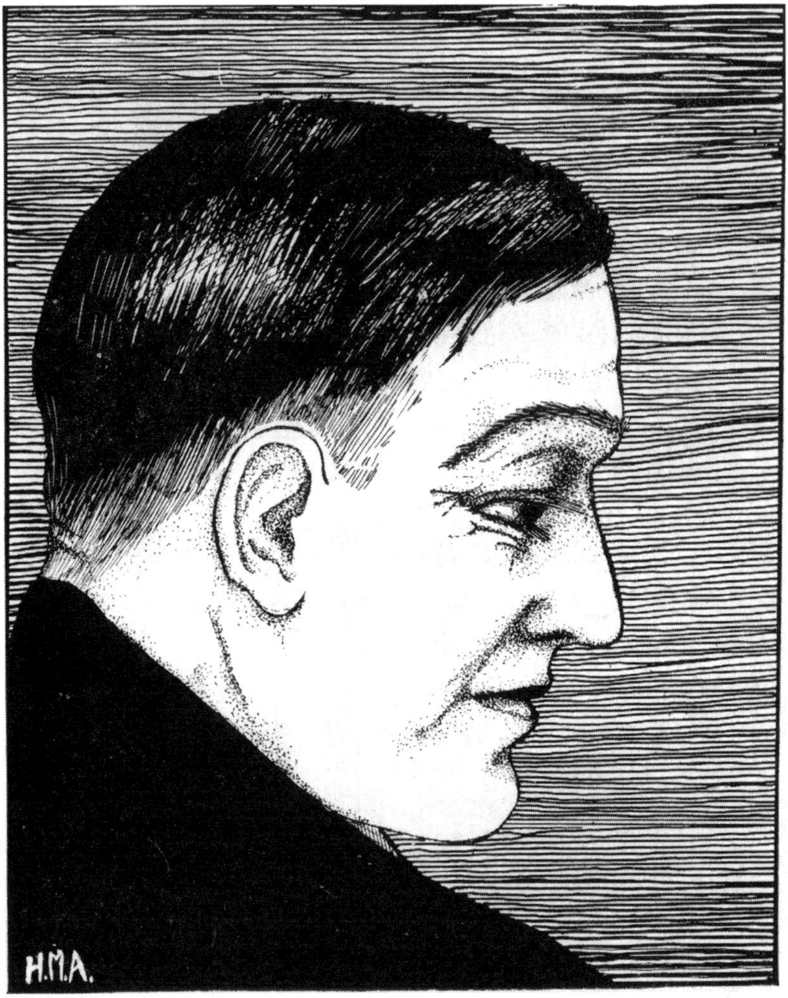

Jay Sigmund. Drawn by Herbert Ainsworth who was associate editor of art for *The Pulse,* February, 1925 issue.

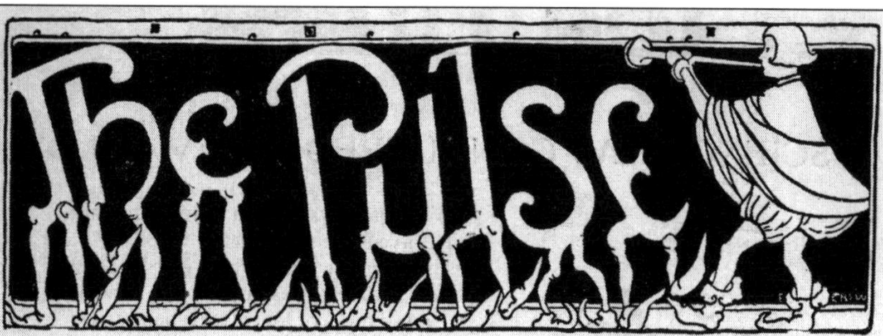

WASHINGTON HIGH SCHOOL, CEDAR RAPIDS, IOWA

Volume XXV **FEBRUARY, 1925** *Number 3*

INTERVIEW WITH MR. SIGMUND

ATTENTION! all ye poets and would be poets!

"Don't put it off! The time to begin writing poetry is during your high school years." So says Mr. Jay Sigmund. Mr. Sigmund is a firm believer that poetry belongs to youth.

Mr. Sigmund is one of Cedar Rapids' prominent business men. His main interest is life insurance, but he takes up writing as a hobby. His office is lined with pictures of famous poets; "For inspiration," he explained, smiling. "I have always wondered," he said, "what it was that came into my life that started me to writing, for it is very unusual for a man of thirty-five to start writing poetry. I never had done much of any writing until 1921. Since then I have written eleven short stories and numerous poems. You can easily tell what kind of writing is most popular, for more people have spoken about my eleven short stories than about all of my poems. But interest in poetry has greatly increased in the last ten years; men like Edgar Guest are partly responsible. Also, after a great emotional upheaval of a nation, like the World War, interest in poetry always increases."

A role model involved in his community. Here's a small portion of an interview with Jay Sigmund in Cedar Rapids Washington's *The Pulse* from February, 1925.

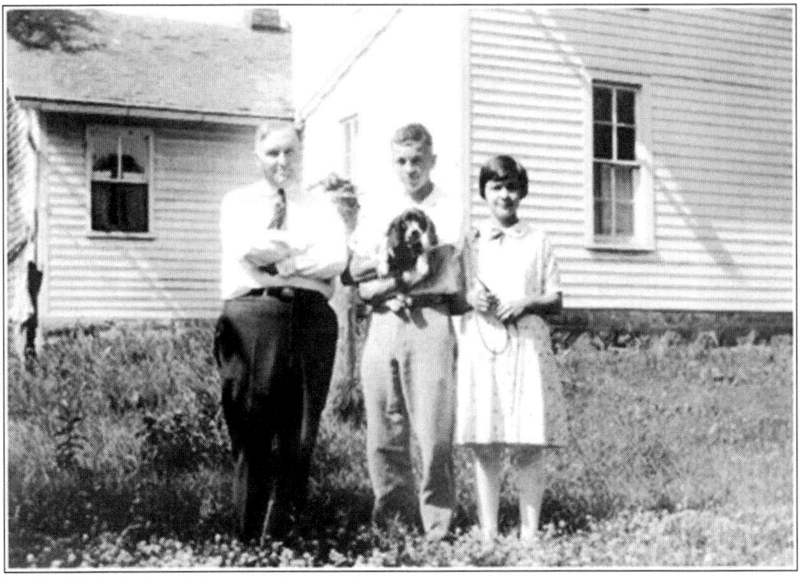

Sigmund and two of his children from the collection of Virginia Sigmund Myers. Circa 1923.

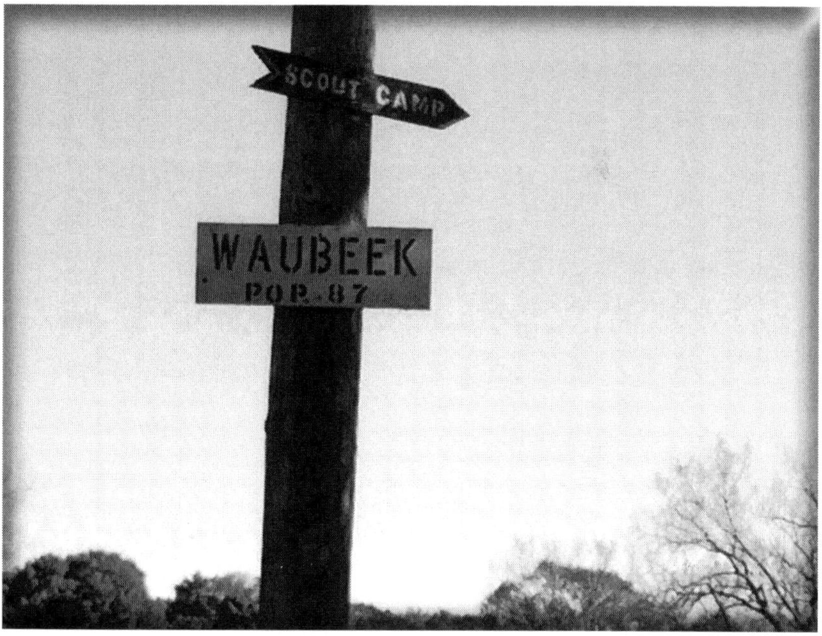

ROAD TO WAUBEEK:

Discovering Jay G. Sigmund

When you think of the history of art in Cedar Rapids, Iowa, you have many angles to plot. You must chart the influences and they do not stop at city limits because influences are never so geographically tidy. You will further discover that these influences sometimes pass up the mansions and stop at the humblest doors of all. Names which are still great and names which mean little today, have left their mark on Cedar Rapids since the earliest days of the twentieth century.[1]

As a former teacher, I was eager to join Mark Hunter in planning The History Center's country school tour. I wanted to learn more about the beginnings of Iowa's well reputed education system and felt sure this program would attract many visitors. I was also excited to add to the Jay Sigmund example for my class on how museums use archived materials.

> Iowa's one-room school houses were landmarks in education. The teachers who taught in them made Iowa a leader in learning and the students left a legacy that remains to this day. Iowans who attended one-room schools include US President Herbert Hoover; the author of *The Little House on the Prairie* series, Laura Ingalls Wilder; America's best-known Regionalist artist, Grant Wood; and an insurance salesman who came to be known as the Poet of the Wapsipinicon Valley, Jay G. Sigmund.[2]

Mark and I began by pouring over old maps of Linn County. Little icons designated many of our county's country schools, but none mentioned Sigmund's Rabbit Grove. We decided to use his letter to Dr. Stookey for clues:

> The place where I was born is a mile south of the village of Waubeek. It was known as the old Rose Bennett farm. I lived there until nine years of age. Then we moved into the village of Waubeek for the winter, then settled on a farm in the vicinity known as Jordan's Grove and when I was about fifteen years old my father bought a farm three miles and a half southeast of Central City on the Wapsipinicon River. It is the Cook's Ford neighborhood as there was a ford in the river at that point. At that time, I went to school, to a country school called the Rabbit Grove School House. Later I went to the Central City Iowa

> High School. I came to Cedar Rapids when I was 19 years of age and did not begin writing until 1921.[3]

Our explorations didn't take us far from downtown Cedar Rapids or far from Interstate 380 and Highway 151. But the countryside made it seem as though we'd entered a completely different world; my first recognition of the beauty of an Iowa landscape. It was easy to imagine one room schools dotting this area in the past and we were successful in finding several of the fifty-four still standing in Linn County.[4]

We saved Waubeek for the end of our search. The bluffs along the peacefully flowing Wapsipinicon River were shrouded in mist. Many of the roads were unpaved. We passed humble stone or clapboard homes, churches, and barns that lent the entire valley a feeling of tranquility. Abandoned farm machinery in the fields seemed to be waiting patiently for the past to return. At a stop in a quiet clearing between Waubeek and Central City we spotted a simple farm storage building. Checking our maps, we realized it was once the Rabbit Grove Country School. Success at last!

Shortly after our return from exploring the area around Waubeek, Ortha Harstad, President of the History Center Board of Directors at the time, asked if I would like to meet Jay Sigmund's daughter-in-law. The two were friends and both lived at Cottage Grove Place, a retirement community in Cedar Rapids, she explained. I had no idea how word of our search had spread so quickly, but I accepted the invitation with pleasure.

Being introduced to Virginia Sigmund Myers was the real turning point on my road to discovery. Mrs. Sigmund-Myers, who insisted I call her "Virginia," was an incredibly gracious

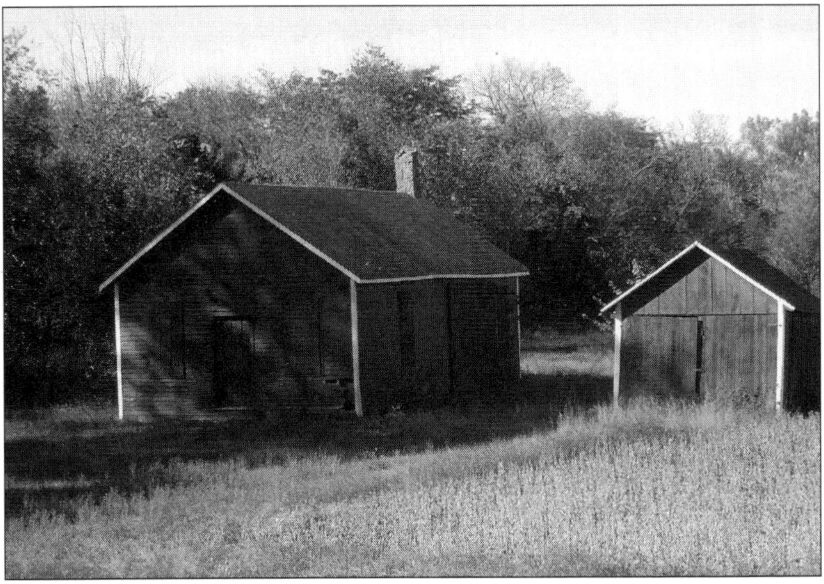

Rabbit Grove school site, 2001

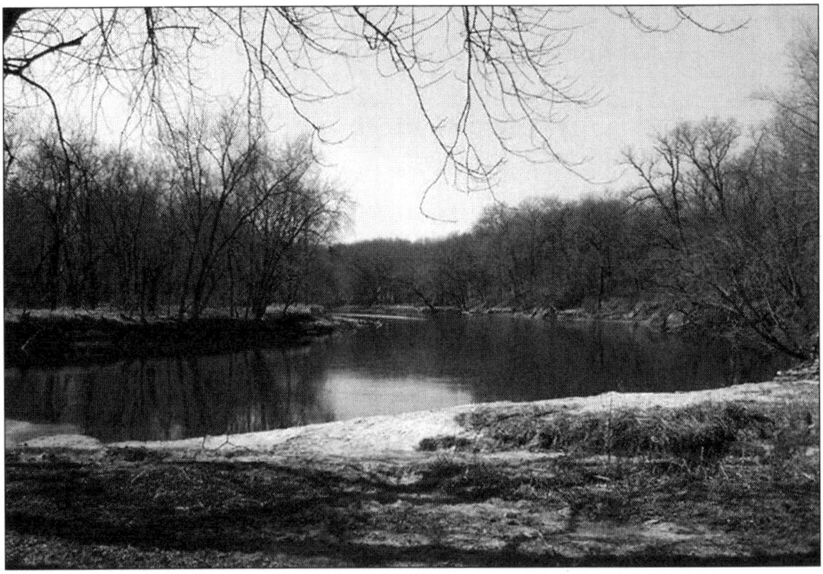

Wapsipinicon River, Waubeek, 2001

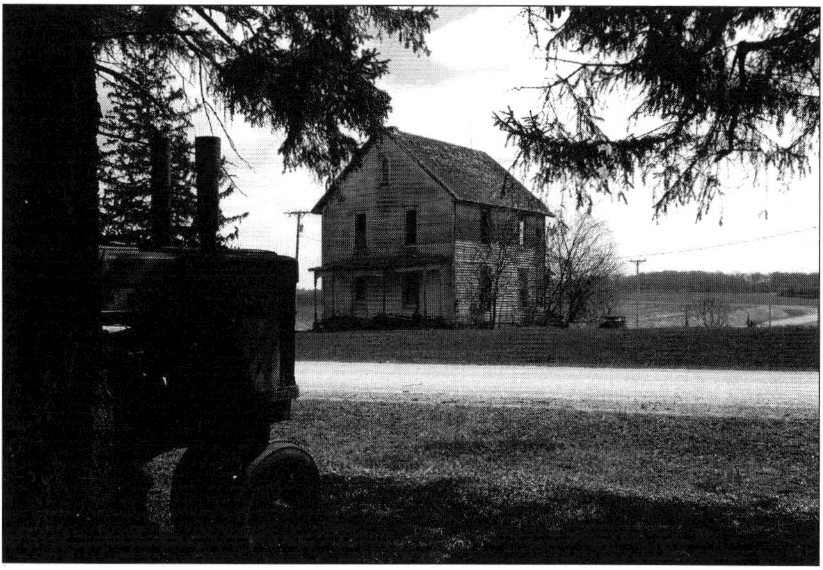

Scene on the way to Waubeek, 2004

ninety-year-old with a quick smile, a great memory, and a wonderful sense of history. Most importantly for me, she idolized Jay Sigmund and was thrilled to share what she knew of his story. Not much time passed before we became friends.

That first night, I joined both Ortha and Virginia at a dinner served in the elegant dining hall of Cottage Grove Place. The conversation was relaxed and friendly. The food was simple but tasty. After our meal, Mrs. Harstad excused herself and went to her apartment while Virginia invited me up to her own residence for continued conversation. She said to make myself comfortable while she brewed some tea. I wandered around her cozy sitting room, gazed at knick-knacks, admired fresh flowers, and looked at the various pieces of art work on her walls. A simple painting of quilts caught my eye. There seemed to be something special about it.

"I don't know much about art," I called to Virginia, "but this painting of quilts interests me. Is it an Impressionist piece?"

"Funny you should ask that," she responded, coming to me with a tray of tea cups in hand. "If you look closely, you'll see the artist's signature."

I could hardly believe my eyes, saying out loud: "Grant Wood!"

"Yes. Come sit over here," she said, indicating a couple of overstuffed chairs around a coffee table. Virginia proceeded to share tea, cakes, and the first of many stories about Jay Sigmund.

"*The Quilts* painting was done in 1928. Grant was in his Impressionist stage at the time and it was my father-in-law who coaxed him out of it...," she began.[5]

That first evening with Virginia I not only learned Grant Wood and Jay Sigmund were close friends, but discovered several other remarkable connections. Sigmund had actually convinced Grant to paint Iowa, which would lead to Wood becoming a world-known Regionalist artist. In later visits, Virginia shared what she called her "treasure chest," an old trunk filled with letters, photographs, newspaper clippings, book reviews, and all types of correspondence between Grant Wood and Jay.

I took the opportunity to ask about one of the photos she showed me. In it, Jay Sigmund was standing between Christopher Morley and Grant Wood, the latter holding a bison horn in his hand. I recognized the photo because a copy was on exhibit at The History Center. I'd quite enjoyed several books written by a Christopher Morley, my favorites being *The Haunted Bookshop* and *Kitty Foyle,* which was the basis for a 1940's movie starring Ginger Rogers. I asked if the Christopher Morley in the photograph

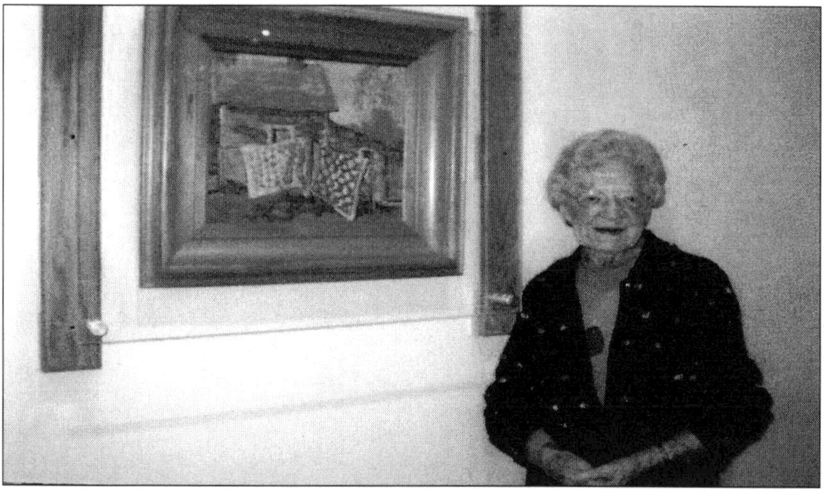

Virginia Sigmund Meyers and the painting *Quilts*. Close up of *Quilts* by Grant Wood, 1928, below.

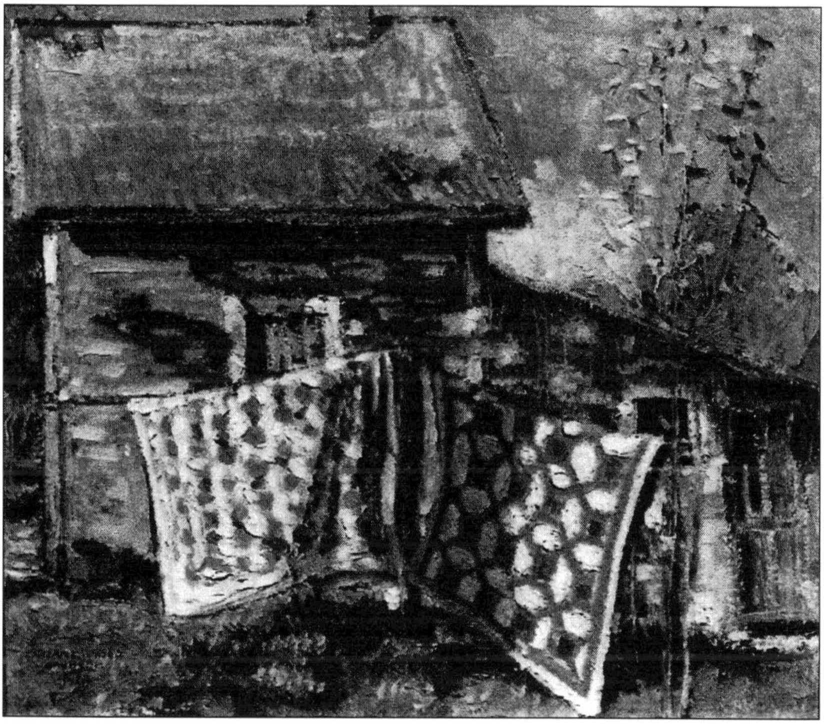

was this same author from New York. (Photo below, Morley, Sigmund, and Wood)

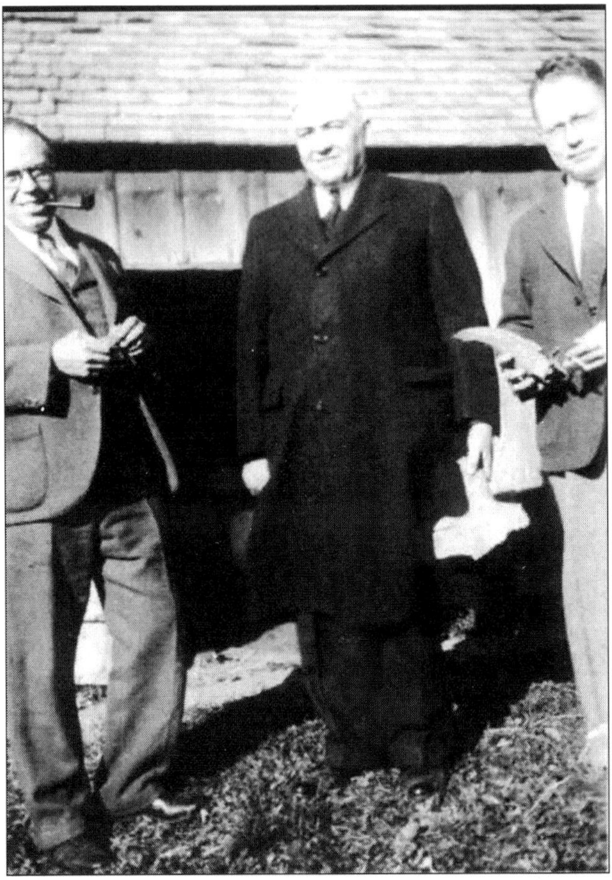

"Oh yes!" Virginia replied. "I took that photo back in 1934 when Christopher Morley visited Waubeek."

"How did Christopher Morley come to visit Waubeek, Iowa?" I asked. "I don't mean to put it down, but the entire village only has a population of eighty-seven!"

Virginia laughed and explained that after the huge success of *American Gothic,* Grant had become rather famous and he was frequently invited to speak to groups across the country.

Iowa City had such a group. The group began as the Saturday Luncheon Club—the Journalism Dinner Club for a season or two, and then the more or less famous Times Club, which met at Smitty's Café.

> On the Times Club: "It is remarkable how easy it was to get the men we most wanted, and for small fees.... We spent unforgettable hours with these visitors of ours. Fixed in my memory is a picture of (Robert) Frost sitting on the small of his back in an easy chair after his talk and his readings, holding a glass of milk in his hand and regaling us between sips with amusing Amherst legends. And (Carl) Sandburg intoning folk songs to the accompaniment of his guitar. And (Sherwood) Anderson gathered with students before a fireplace, chatting, his face in the firelight looking for all the world like that of a nice comfortable old lady. His talk, too, was mild and easy, but his ideas explosive."[6]

"Grant was very shy," Virginia said. "While he agreed to speak, he was pretty uncomfortable at times. After he described some of the trials and tribulations he'd endured, he, Jay, and the founders of the Times Club decided there should be a way to make visitors to Iowa City feel more comfortable. Grant's humorous and artistic sense resulted in the group becoming 'The Society for Prevention of Cruelty to Speakers.'" (See photo on next page). Virginia chuckled at the memory.

"Grant helped them design a very special clubroom above Smitty's Café in Iowa City. I believe Christopher Morley, who was editor of the very popular *Saturday Review of Literature* at that time, was the first guest to enjoy these new quarters."

To enhance an atmosphere of informality, (Frank Luther) Mott and Wood originated the Society for the Prevention of Cruelty to Speakers. A two-room "clubhouse" above Smitty's', consisting of dining and sitting rooms, was obtained rent-free from the owner for the Society and decorated in what Grant Wood described as "the worst style of the late Victorian period." (photo below) Following their talks, refreshments and improvised entertainment in the club house were to amuse and relax such "interesting people" as Stephen Vincent Benet, John Erskine, Mackinlay Kantor, Gilbert Seldes, and Nicholas Roosevelt."[7] [Author note: I later learned Smitty's is where Prairie Lights Bookstore is today.][8]

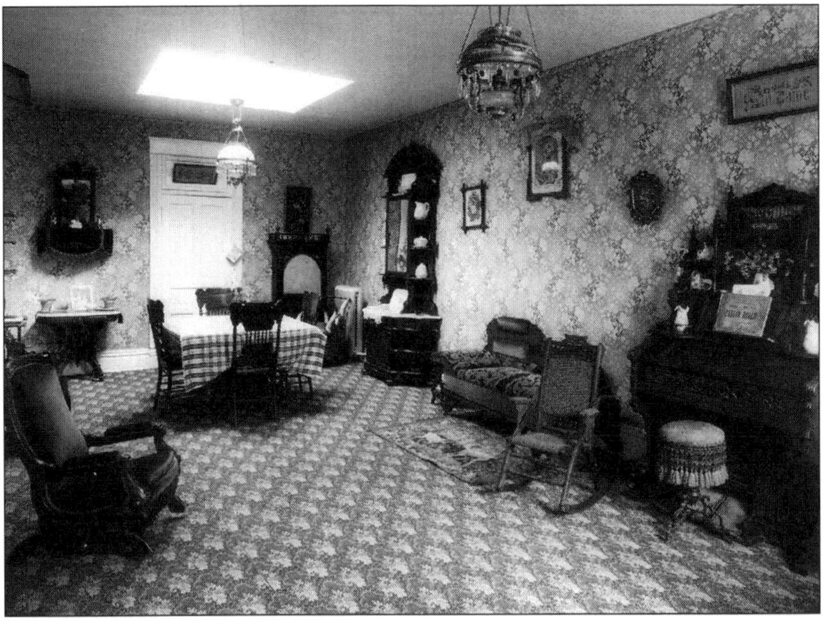

Then, a second revelation was shared. Perhaps because we were speaking of Iowa City, Virginia asked if I knew about Paul Engle (see photo below). "Oh yes!" I responded with enthusiasm. "His International Writing Workshop is even famous in New York, and, I suspect, around the world."

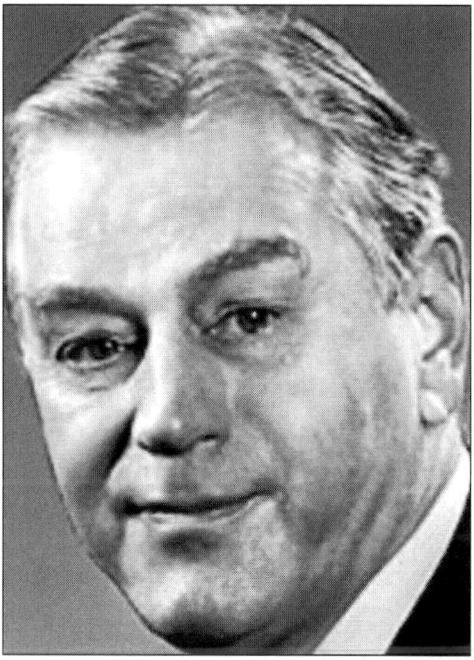

"Well then, you might be interested to know that Paul Engle was Jay Sigmund's paperboy. Jay introduced him to poetry. The rest is history."

> At one house I always took the paper to the door and knocked, because the local poet, Jay Sigmund, lived there.
>
> "Sit down, Paul. I'll read you a new poem."
>
> Jay moved slowly but his eyes moved fast. In the city he kept alive the rural life he knew as a boy along the Wapsipinicon River northeast of Cedar Rapids. In the business world where he spent his days, he made his practical way through actuarial tables, premiums,

> insurance policies, with poems hiding in his pockets like pups waiting to jump out and bark. For him the days were not "all alike as huddled quail." Each one was a new scrutiny of human faces, a sniff at the weather, a stare at the changing air, an ear for the babble of many voices on that round tower of Babel, the earth, rolling through space like an immense monosyllable O.[9]

Virginia's comment, "The rest is history!" was spot on. Paul Engle's poetry led him to become a Rhodes Scholar, a long time and successful director of the Iowa Writers' Workshop at the University of Iowa, and a co-founder, with wife Hualing, of the University of Iowa's world famous International Writing Program.

Of course, many of the stories Virginia shared with me were simply about the Sigmund family itself. She'd married Jay's son Jim, who passed away in the 1960s. Sadly, their one son had also passed away. Jay's older daughter, Mary, died back in 1997. Mary had married Bud Dickey. I knew Bud Dickey. He owned the cleaners I used in Marion. And, before starting at the history museum, I had taught at McKinley Jr. High with Bud and Mary's son Jan. I also knew their daughter Cheri, another retired teacher, who at the time was a volunteer in The History Center archives and was to later work very closely with me at The Granger House Museum in Marion. In other words, I knew two of Jay Sigmund's grandchildren before I'd ever even heard of the poet!

"His younger daughter, Jane Cooper, still lives in Central City," Virginia continued. "We'll have to arrange for you to meet her."

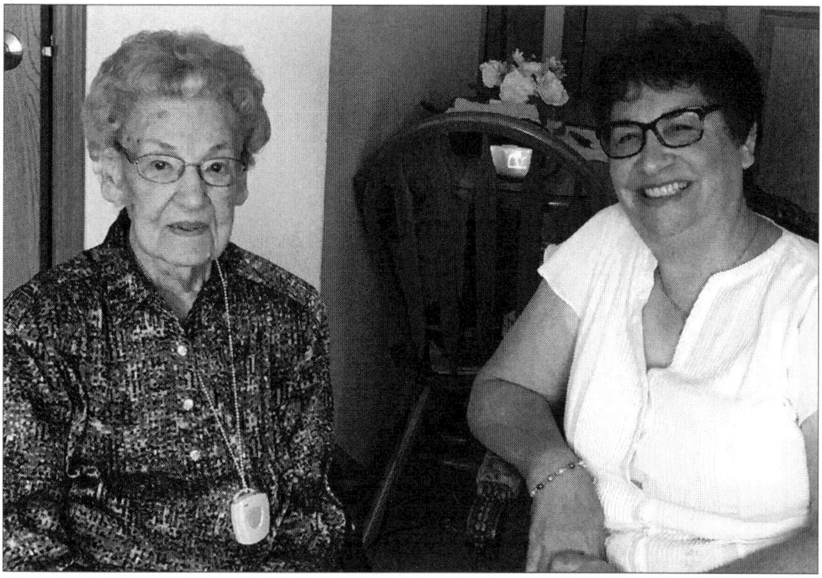

Daughter Jane Sigmund Cooper with author, 2017

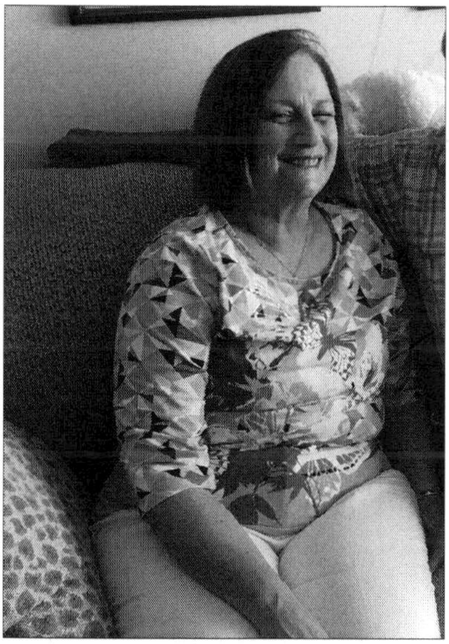

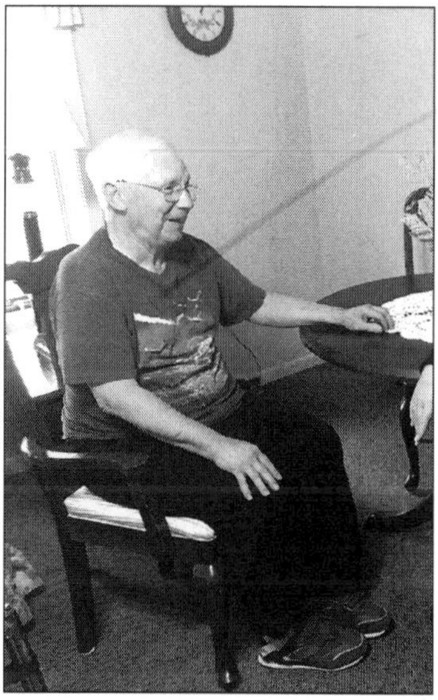

Grandchildren Cheri Dickey (left) and brother Jan.

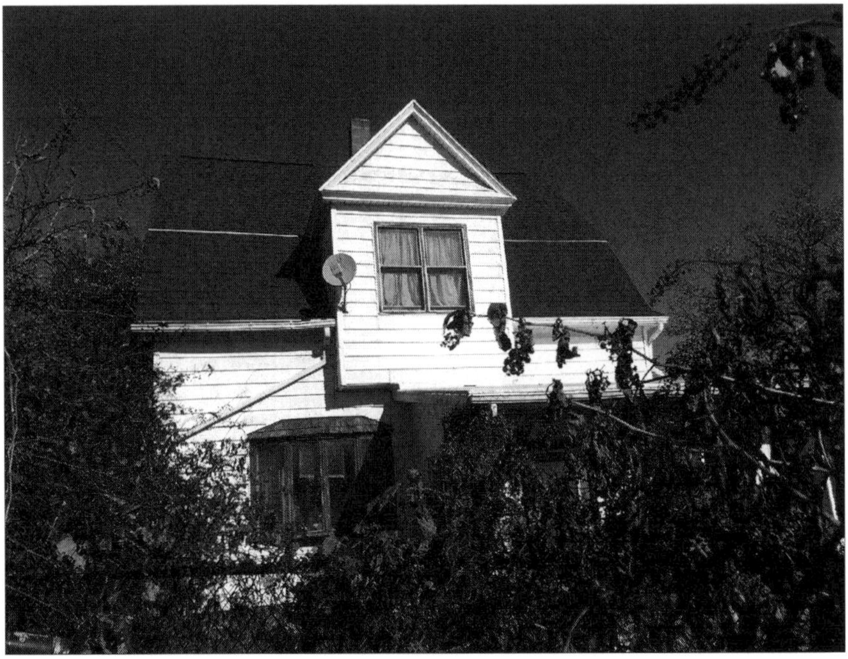

Grant Wood's Waubeek house

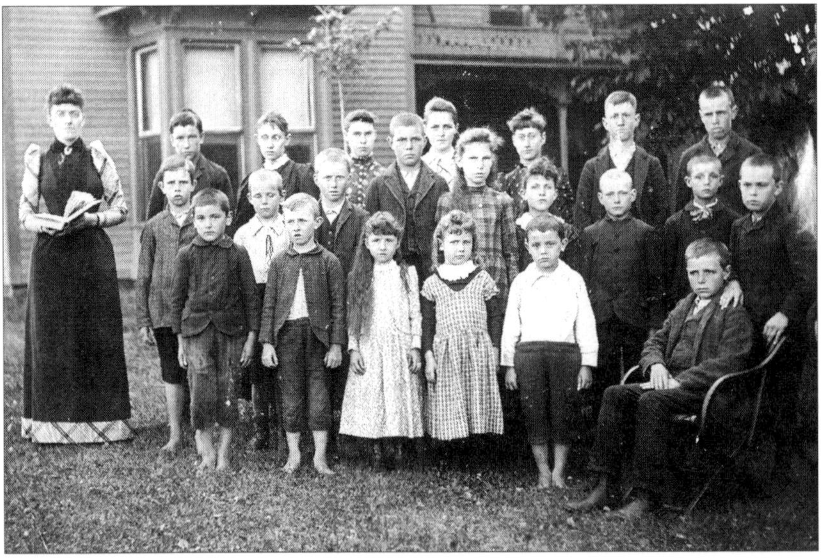

Photo from Cheri Dickey. Sigmund is first on bottom left

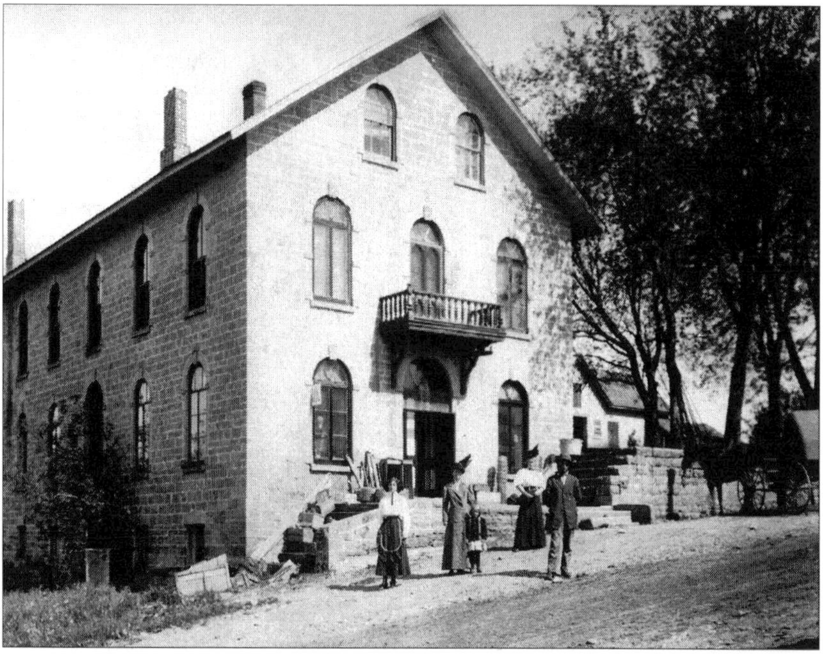

Now FB&Company restaurant, this building, made of Stone City stone has served as Waubeek's centerpiece for over 100 years. Given to the author by restaurant attendant Tracy Schellhorn (owner is Tim Kula)

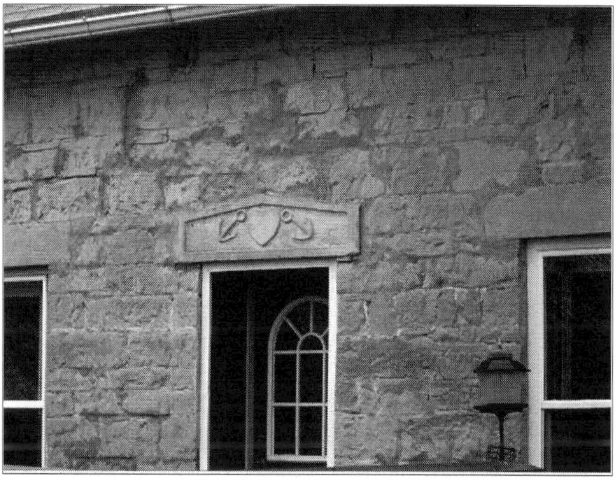

Detail showing the anchors used above the doorway by New England whalers who moved to Waubeek.

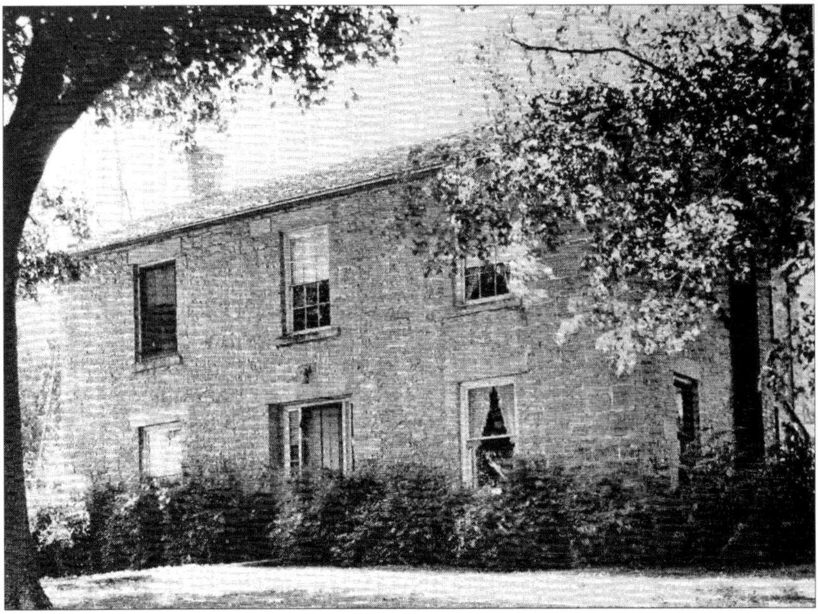

Home in Waubeek which served as a model for Pleasant Hill

With Jan Dickey and Virginia as my guides, I was introduced to Mrs. Cooper and given a personal tour of Waubeek, Iowa. I was taken to Jay Sigmund's birth place and to the house he and his family had used to escape the summer heat of Cedar Rapids. Other highlights included architectural features linking Waubeek to the New England whalers who'd moved there, presumably to get as far away from the ocean as possible. I also was shown the spot where the quilt Grant Wood had painted hung so many years before.

My visit to Waubeek connected Jay Sigmund and Grant Wood in another way. My understanding was that after *American Gothic* had secured his name as an artist, Grant continued working on local decorating projects. What many considered his crowning

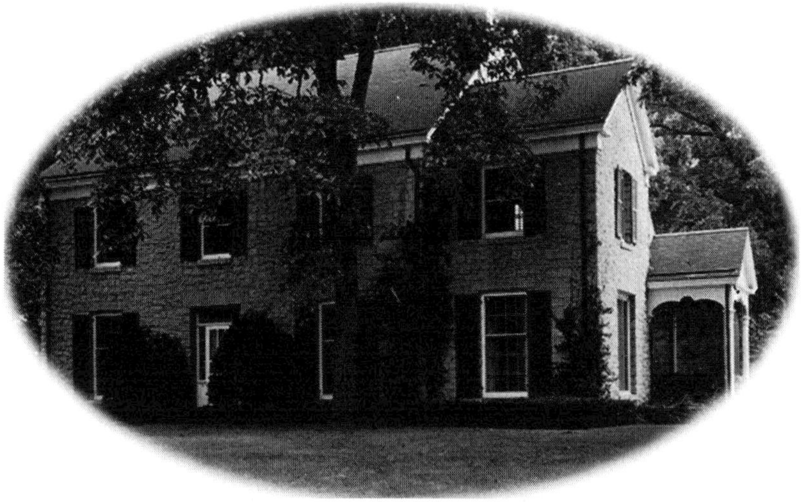

Pleasant Hill.

achievement was a home he and architect Bruce McKay designed and had built for Robert C. and Esther Armstrong. Ultimately called Pleasant Hill, it is now serves as home for Coe College presidents.[10] The design they chose, believe it or not, was based on a house in Waubeek:

> Jay Sigmund, who lived in Waubeek and was a friend to them all (Armstrongs, Wood, and McKay), gave them many historic details about old places. Plans were worked out through their visits to old houses noticing details of paneling, simplicity of fireplace design, wall surfaces, doorways, cornices, chimneys and the general "mass." Esther recalls what a wonderful experience it was for her and for Robert to junket around the countryside with such good company, and such fun.[11]

One summer day in 1934 or 1935, I was sitting in the yard of the Jay G. Sigmund country house talking to my future parents-in-law. The location was Waubeek, an unincorporated village along the Wapsipinicon River in Linn County.

A car drove up and Grant Wood and Esther and Robert Armstrong got out and greeted us. Grant had just taken Robert and Esther to see houses in the area. One stone structure, built in the 1800's had a charm and dignity they loved. The original builder had probably patterned it after many New England homes as that is where many of the settlers came from.

That house became the model for theirs, and was named Pleasant Hill. Just a short time before Robert's death, I asked the Armstrong's if they had ever looked for the house again. Esther said they'd tried but failed to find it. I offered to drive them there which we did one day. As we drove up the lane, I heard Esther say, "Oh, Robert, there's our house!"[12]

My husband, Steve, is a physics professor at Coe College so I was excited to share information about the home of its presidents. Our conversation led me to realize we might have yet another connection to the Jay Sigmund story.

As it happens, Steve runs an undergraduate research group on the study of the atomic structure of glass. Dr. Don Stookey, famous for being the inventor of Corningware, graduated from Coe in 1936 and was in town celebrating seventy years since he'd graduated. During this visit to Cedar Rapids, Dr. Stookey accepted our invitation to have him as a dinner guest in our home. Because I had discovered an original 1934 archival letter from Jay Sigmund, written to a Dr. Stookey of Mechanicsville,

Iowa, I invited Virginia as well. The two got along famously and reminisced about the past. As I'd hoped, it turned out that the Dr. Stookey who wrote the letter that started all my research, was the uncle of the Dr. Stookey who had given glass science such a propitious boost and was sitting in our very house.

So far, I've given you a peek at many connections to Jay G. Sigmund, but I haven't really told you much about the man himself. I think it's time.

Jay was born on December 11, 1885, to Herman and Sarah Jane (Bruce) Sigmund. When his family moved to a farm in Waubeek's Jordon's Grove area, along the Wapsipinicon River, the nine-year-old boy became interested in natural history.

> The soil was sandy and thin, but it proved an excellent breeding ground for box turtles and striped squirrels. I became the envy of the neighborhood because I had a circus in which 5 pet turtles served as a herd of hippopotamus and several ground squirrels I'd caught became tigers.[13]

As already mentioned, young Jay went to Rabbit Grove, a one-room country school house just outside of Waubeek. He later attended Central City High School. Though he, as many of his generation, never graduated, he built a name for himself there.

> When I was about fourteen years old, a chum whose tastes were very similar to mine, saw an advertisement in a magazine for a book called 'How to Stuff Birds and Animals,' the price of which was ten cents. We managed to raise this capital between us and sent

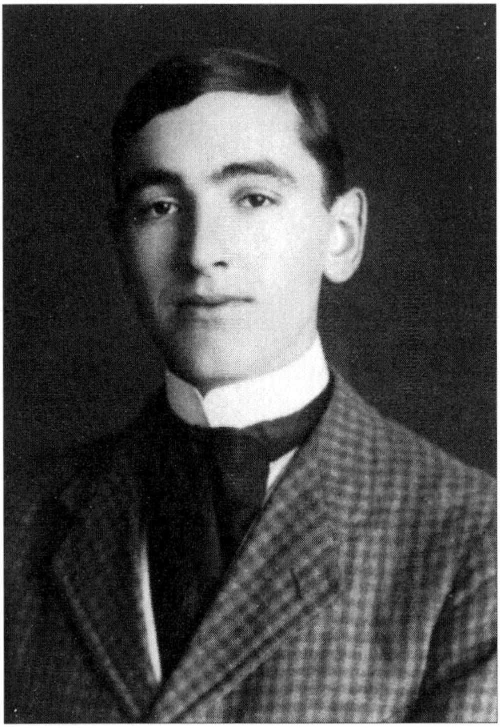

A young Jay Sigmund

> away for the book, owning it in partnership...I started in about this time at Central City High School and became the school's taxidermist. I built quite a little museum of mounted birds and animals in the school, which accounts for my first venture into writing, for a nature magazine devoted entirely to birds.[14]

At nineteen years of age the young man destined to one day become known as the Poet of the Wapsipinicon Valley, moved to the southeast side of Cedar Rapids from his family's farm in Waubeek. Wearing his love of literature on his sleeve, Sigmund immediately became involved with the new Carnegie library project. Papers found in the Special Collections of the University of Iowa Library tell us he was on one of the early Cedar Rapids

Public Library's board of directors and a founding member of the newly incorporated Cedar Rapids Art Association. The special collection's papers also give evidence that Sigmund was very involved with 4-H and the American Boy Scouts, having earned a "second degree membership in the Order of Owls,"[15] (The Order of Owls was a secret fraternal order founded in 1904 in South Bend, Indiana. Its "catechism" said "Owls do good, speak kindly, shake hands warmly, and respect and honor their women."[16])

Jay's first job was unloading sugar for the Warfield, Pratt, and Howell Warehouse. After quitting there, he went into the insurance business, first as a salesman for the Cedar Rapids Life Insurance Company and later its vice president.

On August 9, 1910, he married Louise Bernadine Heins of Cedar Rapids. Together, they had three children: James Bruce

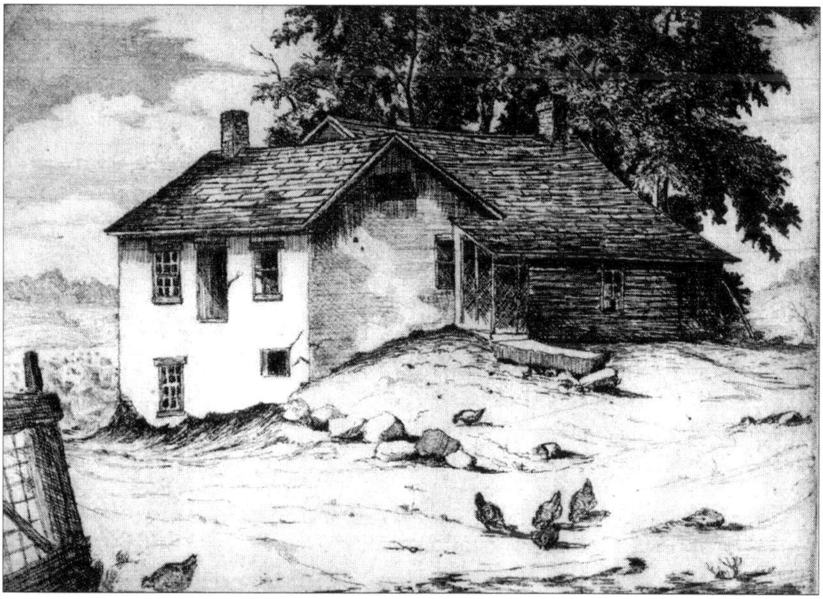

Sketch of Jay's home of birth by Don Glassell

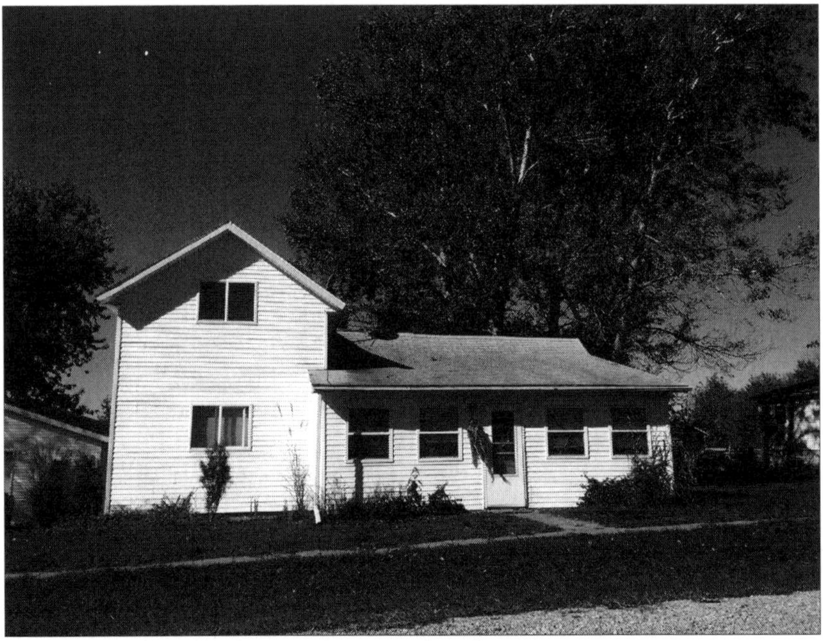

Sigmund family home in Waubeek.

Sigmund, Mary Louise (Mrs. L.D. Dickey), and Jane Elizabeth (Mrs. William Cooper).[17]

As the years passed, Jay remained intimately involved in his new home's cultural community, but he never lost his love for Waubeek and the Wapsipinicon River Valley where he was born. In fact, when the Cedar Rapids Life Insurance Company merged with Mutual of Omaha in 1936, Jay refused a promotion to a presidency position because it would have meant a move to Nebraska.[18]

Around 1920, a small house belonging to family friend Rozela Bennett, the town's mid-wife who had actually delivered Jay Sigmund, came up for sale. Jay purchased it and all its furnishings. Located less than half a mile from the Wapsipinicon River, the family's second home was used extensively as a retreat during warm Iowa summers and for holiday and weekend getaways. With it, rural Linn County permeated their lives.[19] Sigmund's daughter and grandchildren remember the Waubeek home fondly:

> JANE COOPER (DAUGHTER): Our house was across from the church. It was owned by a midwife named Rozela Bennett. Dad bought it from her. Have you heard her name?
>
> BARB FELLER (AUTHOR): Oh yes, your father mentions her in the letter to Dr. Stookey that is in the archives of The History Center.
>
> JANE (TO GROUP): She delivered my Dad and his sister. This was in a smaller out building on her land.
>
> BARB: We could see her farm on the map.
>
> JAN DICKEY (GRANDSON): That's the house we visited.
>
> BARB: Yes. I have a scan of a sketch of it. I found pages and pages online about the artist who sketched it.
>
> JAN: That would be Don Glassell. I believe there is a water color of it as well. Wasn't it hanging in Grammy's house?
>
> JANE: Don's wife Chris was also an artist. These artists were mostly pretty poor. Don and Chris didn't have any insurance. So Don took out a policy with my dad and paid by giving him these sketches and paints.
>
> BARB: I believe there's now an entire gallery devoted to Don's work in the Museum of Art in Dubuque.[20]

JANE: Dad bought the main house from Mrs. Bennett after he moved to town. [Cedar Rapids] Maybe it was after she was widowed?

VIRGINIA: I'm not sure.

LARRY COOPER (GRANDSON): Grandpa died before we were born, but we grandkids remember the house. There was no indoor plumbing, a well, an outhouse, no electricity. It was rustic! We even used kerosene lamps and slept on mattress ticks filled with corn-husks.

VIRGINIA: Hardly any of those farms had electricity until the `30s.

CHERI DICKEY (GRANDDAUGHTER): It wasn't quite a cabin. It was more like a small house. It was in a shaded space with lots of land behind it. First floor had a dining room, kitchen, living room, and bed-room. Upstairs had two more bedrooms. And there was a barn.[21] It was kind of like Granger House.[22]

JANE: Everything was left as it was, furniture, dishes, and all. I even remember there was a spinning wheel in one corner.

VIRGINIA: And I remember an Indian beaded vase, ornamental, that hung on the wall.

JANE: It was fun for us to get out in the country and do things we'd never done before.[23]

Jay, who had always enjoyed being outdoors, would arrange frequent excursions for his young family. While hiking along the Wapsipinicon they would learn to identify animal tracks, leaves, plants, and birds. Many times, they'd also come across Native American artifacts.

> JAN: I remember there were lots of artifacts in the house in Waubeek. They were in a large square case with shelves.
>
> JANE: Dad was also a great nature lover. We used to go walking along the river in Waubeek and he'd always take us to the sand hill to look for arrowheads. I never will forget, one weekend when we were up there, he came back from his walk all excited. He had seen an "oven bird"[24] nest and he wanted us to see it. And how he found his way back through that timber right to that nest I'll never know. But there it was, a little plain nest just like a little lemon and that was the only time I've ever seen one of them.
>
> BARBARA: How old were you then?
>
> JANE: I think I was about seven. It was the first time I ever had gone fishing, any of us, I guess. [Referring to brother and sister.] We walked up to this little pond called "Bullhead Pond." And he bought us all cane poles and straw hats and overalls. We'd never had a pair of overalls in our life, but he'd leave 'em there and we would wear them on weekends, just like everybody in town did.
>
> BARB: Did you catch anything?
>
> JANE (LAUGHS): Not much. But bull heads. Did catch quite a few bullheads!

Realizing how little he knew about the indigenous residents of the land, Sigmund made an effort to learn more. An avid reader, he delved into Native American lore even in his youth,

Waubeek

"The Wawbeek," said the chanting copper men,
The black rock, it is magic, it can kill!"
Stark cliffs of limestone awed the fiercest brave
And stripped the very sachems of their skill.

But when the paler men came pressing on,
To put the lynx and timber wolf to rout,
They laid their hearths upon these very bluffs
Where evil spirits long had roamed about.

They set the sills which built their house of prayer
Upon the solid blocks, the Wawbeek gave;
They crushed the crag of black rock with their steel
And made the very heart of it their slave.

Old Mudjekeewis, jelaous of his winds
And brooding at the gateway of the west
Was awed to see the pale-face prosper well
Upon the fatal Wawbeek's stony crest.

"My winds have failed to batter down these slopes
And I am short of breath and weak of hand...
Oh, it is hard to watch the white ones come
And grind the fatal Wawbeek into land!"[27]

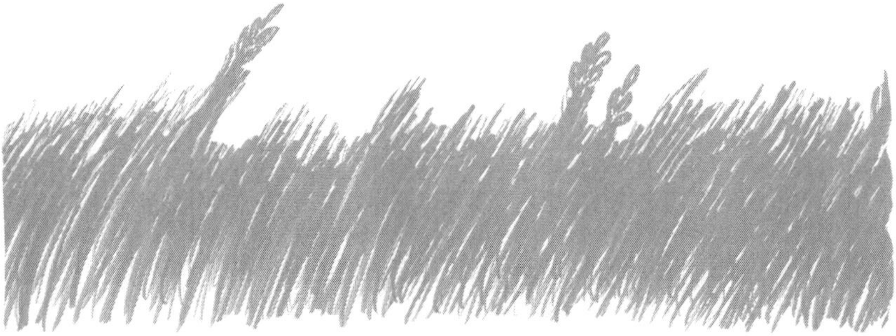

perhaps becoming especially interested when he noted the term "Wawbeek" being used repeatedly in Henry Wadsworth Longfellow's 1855 poetic *Song of Hiawatha*.[25]

> The beautiful little village of Waubeek, on the banks of the Wapsipinicon River in the northeast part of Linn County, takes its name from the limestone cliffs and quarries about it. In Longfellow's poem, *Song of Hiawatha*, is to be found frequent reference to the Fatal Wawbeek or Black Rock. Hiawatha's father, Mudjekeewis, ruler of the winds of heaven, says in answer to Hiawatha's query as to whether there was anything of which the grizzled brave was afraid: "Nothing but the black rock yonder, Nothing but the fatal Wawbeek!"[26]

Using Longfellow's story as his guide, Sigmund wrote the poem "Waubeek."

Probably because most of the more technical references available to him would have dealt with tribes of the Southwest, he decided his outdoor classroom would have to become hands-on. Dubbed by friends and neighbors a weekend archaeologist, Jay collected, recorded, and researched the many objects he and his family found.[28]

Sigmund was very moved by one particular story he learned of. In 1851, a series of treaties between the federal government and various Native American nations had removed most Native Americans from Iowa. In 1856, after nearly ten years of living on a reservation in east central Kansas, a small group of Mississippi Meskwaki-Sauk (Sac and Fox) pooled money from the sale of their horses and personal items, and succeeded in purchasing a piece of land in Tama County, Iowa. Nearly destroyed through

Arrow-Head

Speak, arrow-head!
I would hear your story
I would hear of the part you played
In the great drama which man calls history
What followed, year on year,
Oh, arrow-head?
Or is your voice as silent
As the stern flint from which the young buck fashioned you?
A tombstone immortal...
With its inscription erased
By the mocking hand of Time.[32]

long years of battles and oppression, the Meskwaki-Sauk emerged to live again on Iowa soil.[29]

The more Sigmund immersed himself in the cultural history and beliefs of his American native neighbors, the more he identified with these people who shared his love of the land. *They came from our own soil.*[30] Jay began sharing their stories with scout troops, 4-H clubs, school children, and conservation groups.[31] A writer at heart, Jay wanted to record these tales in a more permanent way. He decided to put his thoughts in poetic form.

Beginning with speculation about who made and used an arrowhead he'd found, and ending in a lamentation for the silent shrouding of the American Indian's past, Sigmund wrote the poem "Arrow-Head."

Continuing his interest in this theme, Sigmund attempted to dramatize a legend of the naming of the Wapsipinicon River. The story of star-crossed lovers is much like that of Romeo and Juliet. Sigmund prefaced his never-published manuscript with these comments:

> "Many and varied are the legends about the beautiful Wapsipinicon River which diagonally bisects the State of Iowa. Probably the most fascinating one, and a tale which has almost become a folk story of the people as well, is the narrative unfolded in this tiny poetic drama...Wapsi and Pinicon, daughter and son of the chieftains of enemy tribes, conducted clandestine meetings along the banks of the lovely river that flowed between their homes. Discovered one evening and forbidden to see each other again, they formed a suicide pact, leaped into the waters and were drowned. The river which provided their watery grave was named the Wapsipinicon."[33]

Anamosa

Her step was silent as the river mist—
She walked where weeping Wapsie walked before
Above the crags to keep midnight tryst
And meet brave Pinicon along the shore.

Oh fair White Fawn, what secret did you know?
What distant river cavern made you home?
You blest the hills; our river down below...
You spoke your benediction to the loam.

Oh lithe White Fawn, the mystic spell you gave
Has wakened men and cheered them at their toil.
May giant white-oaks bend above your grave,
With spreading timber ferns to shade the soil.

And may the harebells, when the drifts have run,
Be blooming in the valley where you like;
May the first rays of springtime's mellow sun
Send down their gentle strokings from the sky.[34]

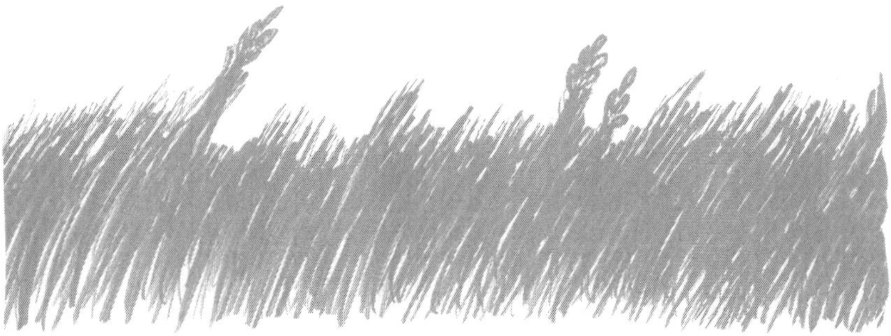

Though the drama remained unpublished, several of Sigmund's poems contained allusions to the legend.

Later, noting that the city of Anamosa was called Lexington until "a very charming Native American maiden" bearing the name Ana-mo-sah (White Fawn) stopped overnight and left her lyric name to delight the ears of those who labored in the Wapsipinicon Valley, Sigmund preserved this legend in his poem, "Anamosa."

If today's avid readers, and even those who have lived most of their lives in Iowa, were asked to list popular authors of the 1920's, names such as Sinclair Lewis, F. Scott Fitzgerald, and Ernest Hemingway, would probably make the list. Jay G. Sigmund probably would not. In actuality, however, many American readers and critics of the time were devoting their attention to an outburst of small, individualistic periodicals that came to be known as "little magazines." Usually their issues were physically small and most of them represented the voices of individual editors or small groups. Their essence was discovery and added to the nation's diversity. Many of those whose writings appeared in these little magazines caught the attention of editors from large publishing firms in Chicago, New York, and across the continent. Thus, little magazines brought new-born awareness to life in Midwest America. In fact many believe:

> "In their pages, where regionalism was born and reared, lies the clearest revelation of the major issues involved in regional theory."[35]

The Wapsipinicon

Oh Wapsie, does your shadow walk
Along this river as the moon
Hangs, sickly pale above the bluffs
When winds of harvest sigh and croon?

And does your lover, Pinicon,
Come back on osprey wings to ride
With silver flight among the mists
When winter's wrath is satisfied?

How fitting that your thwarted love
Be buried where such beauty stays
For what a restful tomb is one
Encompassed by cool waterways![37]

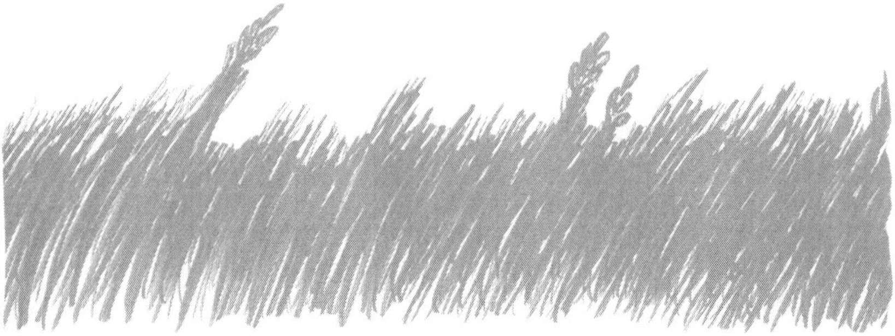

Drunken Land Owner

He feels the breeze that fans the linden bloom
And welcomes it against his throbbing head:
His bleating her are waiting to be fed...
He staggers with his lantern through the gloom.

The cock that greets the morning by its call,
Mocking the sunrise with a beating wing,
Flaps from its roost to watch this sodden thing
Scratch with his pitchfork in a littered stall.

Bleary of eye he sees the calf and sheep
Crunching their clover at the fodder rack
And with a leaden step he totters back
To rouse his sweat-marked horses from their sleep.

Under the sun of noon he plods along
Blind to the sky's blue bowl which roofs his field...
Only concerned with what his loam will yield...
Deaf to the mating vesper sparrow's song.

Watching with jealous eye the mouse and bug;
Striving to coax the corn-sprouts from the soil;
Restless, until the fruitage of his toil
Returns to mock him from an earthen jug![38]

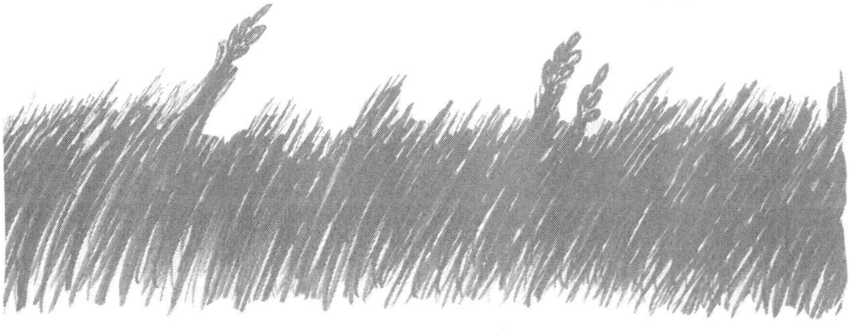

Because Sigmund's simple romantic depictions of Native American legends paralleled the trends of the time—in which metropolitan culture was threatening folk culture— Sigmund struck a chord that ultimately reverberated across the nation. This being a period in which many Americans were experiencing a heightened awareness of native culture, Sigmund's timing was perfect. His first poems, published in local newspapers, attracted the attention of editors across the Midwest and beyond. They appeared in the *Cedar Rapids Republican,* the *Rock Island Argus,* the *Cincinnati Times Star,* the *Davenport Times,* the *Chicago Post* and the *Springfield* [Massachusetts] *Republican.*[36]

Within one year, his works were chosen to appear in *The Anthology of Magazine Verse* for 1922. Its well-known editor, literary critic William Stanley Braithwaite, induced Sigmund to write a book. The resulting *Frescoes* was published in the fall of 1922.

> "Former Central City boy, Jay G. Sigmund, now vice-president of the Cedar Rapids Life Insurance Company, will realize one of his life's ambitions with the publication of his first book of poems, *Frescoes.* Mr. Sigmund has achieved a national reputation. He was born on a farm 36 years ago, near Waubeek. It is one of the wildest, most beautiful portions of Iowa. Just the place where a kid with imagination, a great power of observation and an inspiration to tell what he saw and what he dreamed would find the natural material to be woven into fabric of delicacy and beauty. He loved the flowers, the trees, and the birds...a gatherer of Indian lore and legend.
>
> Now, Vice President of Cedar Rapids Life Insurance, he loves literature and has learned to put the stuff that his best dreams are made of into perfect rhythm

The Bankrupt Farmer's Auction

It seems the township's populace has come
Entire, to this farmer's auction sale:
Some come to gossip—some to gape and jibe;
Some have in mind the cheese and crackers stale
With which to gorge themselves, at call for lunch;
They group together in a motley bunch.

Some come in fur coats like great grizzly bears,
While others dress for this occasion rare;
They've stopped en route and paid their homage to
The village barber and his shears snipped hair
From tousled heads, and then to further preen,
New shirts of flannel and neckties are seen.

You ask me of that farmer over there—
Who is he that he keeps so much apart?
You wonder why he wears this solemn mien
And seems impatient for the sale to start,
Ah this for him and his much faded wife,
Marks a new chapter in their book life!
For soon as exiles they must leave this spot;
Look—in the window pressed against the pane—
A woman's face, deep etched with lines of care;
All of her years of toil now seem in vain.
Small wonder that she fails to hide that tear—
As rings the jargon of the auctioneer![42]

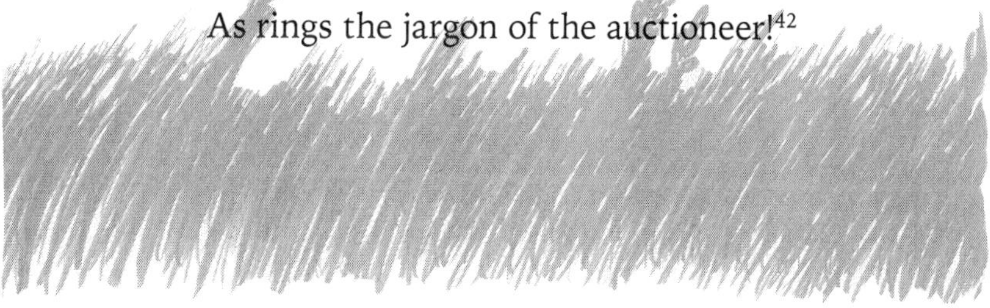

> and often mellifluous rhyme. That's why the best of the critics have praised him and accorded him a place among the best of modern American poets."[39]

In 1923, when Sigmund published his second volume of poetry, *Pinions,* the following ad appeared:

> "When Jay G. Sigmund's first volume of verse, *Frescoes,* appeared last year, this poet was known only to a small circle of people who were readers of certain exclusive poetry magazines, or who chanced to come within the range of the few newspapers that were printing his work. Now his second book, *Pinions,* is eagerly awaited by poetry lovers all over the country, for the leading critics of the United States have been warm in their praise."[40]

In 1928, the Maizeland Press in Des Moines published forty-nine poems by Iowans. Jay G. Sigmund was among them. At this same time, the English Club of Cornell College was publishing a series of Iowa chapbooks edited by Clyde Tull. Sigmund's poetry and short stories could be found here as well.[41]

Considered by some to be foremost in its influence was *The Midland,* published in Iowa City. Its editors, John Fredrick, founder, and Frank Luther Mott, spoke eloquently for the rural preference throughout the eighteen years of its publication—key years in honing Iowa's Regionalism.

The Midland's pages sparkled with the early works of some Iowans destined to win national fame, including Ruth Suckow, Phil Strong, Paul Engle, and MacKinlay Kantor.[41] They ran their journal on the assumption that "Perfection consists in being assimilated into and being in harmony with the natural environ-

Retired

His bare feet came to know the furrow soon
And soon his palms were curved to grasp a hoe;
His ear was tuned to catch the cock's first call...
His back was corded well that it might bend
To move along about a weedy row.

Choosing a mate, he sought no comely form
But looked for one to sweep his kitchen floor;
He wanted one with hands to knead coarse bread—
One with firm knees to grip a milk-pail's flanks
And strength to carry water to his door.

Now his broad acres spread and ripple off,
Marked by the lines of marching corn and cane:
Great barns are hunched above his mounds of hay...
Fat cattle stand and low at feeding time....
His hills are greening from their gifts of rain.

But he is gone and some drab village street
Each day is conscious of his restless tread;
Mutely he plods throughout his taskless day
Or sits beside his somber, toothless mate,
Letting time glide above his weathered head.[47] [48]

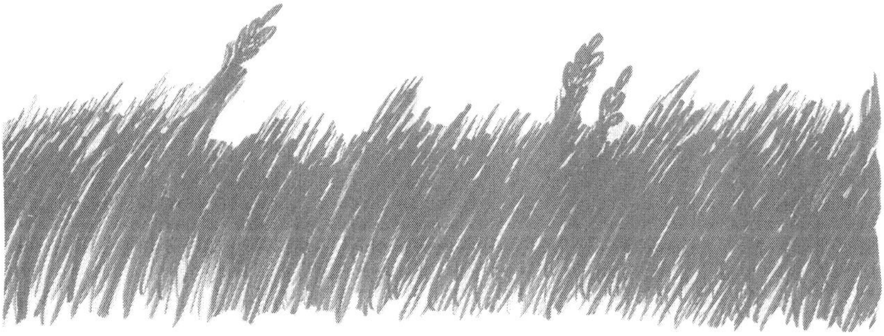

Retrospect

There's many things that I miss
Since it's gone dry;
I'm willin' to admit
Booze was a curse:
But lots of things folks do
Since whisky's gone
It seems to me is
Just as bad—or worse:
'Tain't always drinking booze
That brings a hearse.

A man can kill himself
With too much meat;
Or too much starchy stuff
Will kill him, too;
Meat is a blessin' if
It's rightly used—
So is good booze in
Case of chills or flu,
For run down systems look
What beer can do!

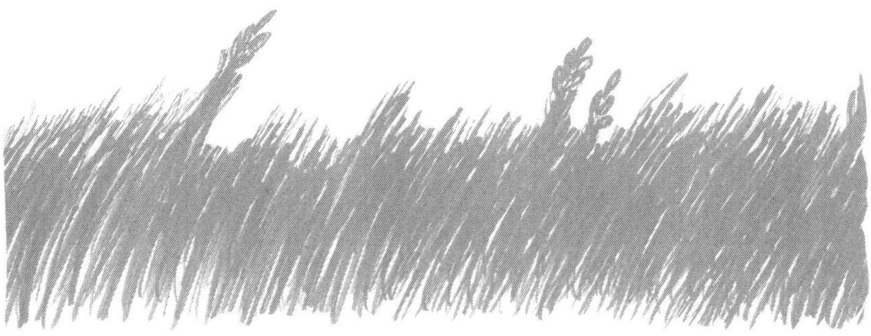

I s'spose there was no doubt
Saloons were bad;
Yet, I won't' think of them
As dens of vice:
To me they always seemed
Like pilgrim's shrines,
Where kindred spirits
Met to swap advice
And treat their souls to joys
Right off of ice!
The thing I miss most is
The social side;
The bully chaps you met
Across the bar:
The sympathy they gave
In times of need,
The words of council
You could carry far,
Them times they set 'em up
With old Three Star![49]

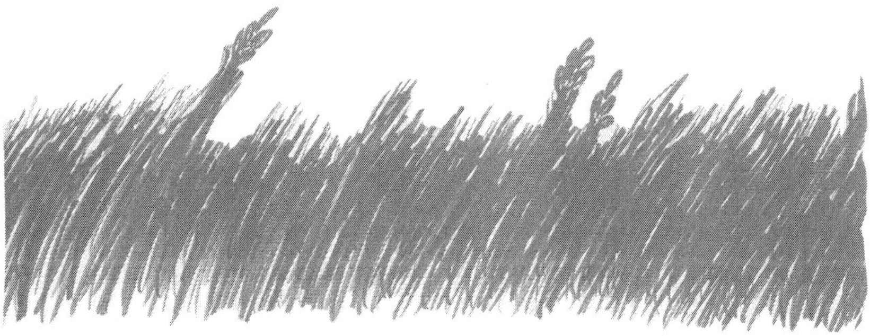

ment." The writings of Jay G. Sigmund personified this image and made him one of the journal's top contributors.[44]

> "If I were asked to mention a writer in whose work I find fully represented all that is racy and authentic in Iowa life, all that is specifically Iowan, I should think of Sigmund at once. Both in his verse and his prose he has achieved, as it seems to me, significant and living characters and situations."[45]

A factor that helped *The Midland* attract good writers was the consistent support of Edward J. O'Brien, who, in 1915, began the compilation of his year-book *Best Short Stories*. In the introduction to his first volume, O'Brien wrote of *The Midland*:

> *Since the most brilliant days of the New England men of letters, no such hope has proclaimed itself with such assurance and modesty.*[46]

Sigmund's poem "Retired" came out in *The Midland* in 1924 and was published a year later in Sigmund's book *Drowsy Ones*.

In *Pinions* and the following two volumes of verse (*Land O'Maize Folk*, 1924; and *Drowsy Ones*, published in 1925) Sigmund continued sharing his love of the natural environs of the Wapsipinicon Valley by introducing his readers to the folk who peopled the region, simultaneously establishing a new theme—poems which began to reflect the plague of problems being experienced by Iowa's farmers for whom the Depression Era had an early beginning.

Pinions opened with a grouping of poems called "Five Corn-Belt Village Portraits" and went on to include such titles as: "Plowman's Chant," "A Harelipped Child," "My Neighbor," and "A Gray Haired Bard Speaks." I find his poem "The Bankrupt

Farmer's Auction" a particularly moving example of Sigmund's feelings.

Land O'Maize Folk was devoted in its entirety to people with sections entitled "Mississippi River Village Folk," "Hillside Folk," and "Yesteryear Folk."[48]

Both *Pinions* and *Land O'Maize Folk* were published by the James T. White Company, New York. *Drowsy Ones,* which came out in 1925, was the first to be published in Cedar Rapids. Its title came from an old school history:

> "And they called this land 'Iowa' which is the Indian name for 'Drowsy Ones.'[50] Seemed quite mournful with such poems as "Drunken Land Owner," "Hill Soul's Death" and "Harvest after Drought."[51]

California poet, Robinson Jeffers, after reading *Drowsy Ones,* wrote to Sigmund, "You have fine powers of observation and imaginative sympathy, as well as a musical verse, and you see keenly and objectively."[52] Meanwhile, American historian, philosopher and literary critic Louis Mumford wrote of Jay: "Your poetry gives one a rich and satisfactory sense of the mid-American earth, and I rejoice in it."[53]

In 1925, Jay Sigmund was featured on the first page of Cedar Rapids' Washington High School's *The Pulse* with a poem and interview:

> Attention all ye poets and would be poets!
>
> Don't put it off! The time to begin writing poetry is during your high school years. So says Mr. Jay Sigmund.
>
> Mr. Sigmund is a firm believer that poetry belongs to youth.

Mr. Sigmund is one of Cedar Rapids prominent business men. His main interest is life insurance, but he takes up writing as a hobby. His office is lined with pictures of famous poets. "For inspiration," he explained, smiling."[54]

Sigmund expanded his theme when he began writing short stories. Four volumes resulted: *Wapsipinicon Tales*, 1927; *Merged Blood*, 1929; *The Ridge Road*, 1930; and *The Least of These*, 1935. The interest in his short stories was as full of praise as for his poetry:

> "Much of the same quality which has distinguished his poetry is to be found in the stories which make up this volume. Of eighteen stories listed by Edward J. O'Brien all are given stars which means that no story has come from this author's pen in two years that did not have qualities of distinction."[55]
>
> "His books are crammed with characters created out of his full knowledge of human traits. He recognized meanness with goodness, and he knew that most have a portion of each...There is in all his work an utterly true perception, whether of human feeling or the weather."[56]
>
> "In literature, Sigmund understood that the blending of people, culture, and nature into an organic unity created and authenticated both folk and regional society. Sigmund fretted that increasing technology separated farmers from their horses and, in the final analysis, distanced them from the soil. His fear of urban growth and the accompanying decline of rural influence permeated many of his works...suggesting that the relentless march of modernization was threatening the entire existence of an earlier Iowa."[57]
>
> "In the short story, he was able to give more attention to his interest in character. Much as Sigmund loved

the Iowa farming country, he could not romanticize it, for he knew how bitter and grinding a job the farmer has, how sometimes no amount of sweat and hard work will make up for bad luck or bad judgment. He understood how farms are lost, go out of the family and are sold by the auctioneer… *Merged Blood* is a collection of short stories not altogether pleasant but representative of the unusual flavor that differs from the common run."[58]

As had been the case for many Iowans, the state's most famous artist to be, Grant Wood, was well acquainted with *The Midland* magazine. He enjoyed reading the works it contained and took special interest in pieces written by Jay G. Sigmund. It is not known how the two actually met (probably through the Cedar Rapids Art Association) but before long, they entered into a close, and what would go on to be, life-long friendship.[59]

When Grant Wood, who had traveled several times to Europe in search of finding his own personal artistic style, spent parts of the summers of 1927 and 1928 in Waubeek, Sigmund took him hiking along the Wapsipinicon River. Their treks and accompanying conversations rekindled Wood's interest in his own rural Iowa roots. Sigmund chided Grant for copying European styles and painting foreign scenes. He advised his friend to stay home and paint what he knew best: Iowa.[60]

"Jay's son, Jim, and daughter-in-law Virginia, told of a time at Waubeek when Grant was visiting in the Sigmund home. They were sitting on the front

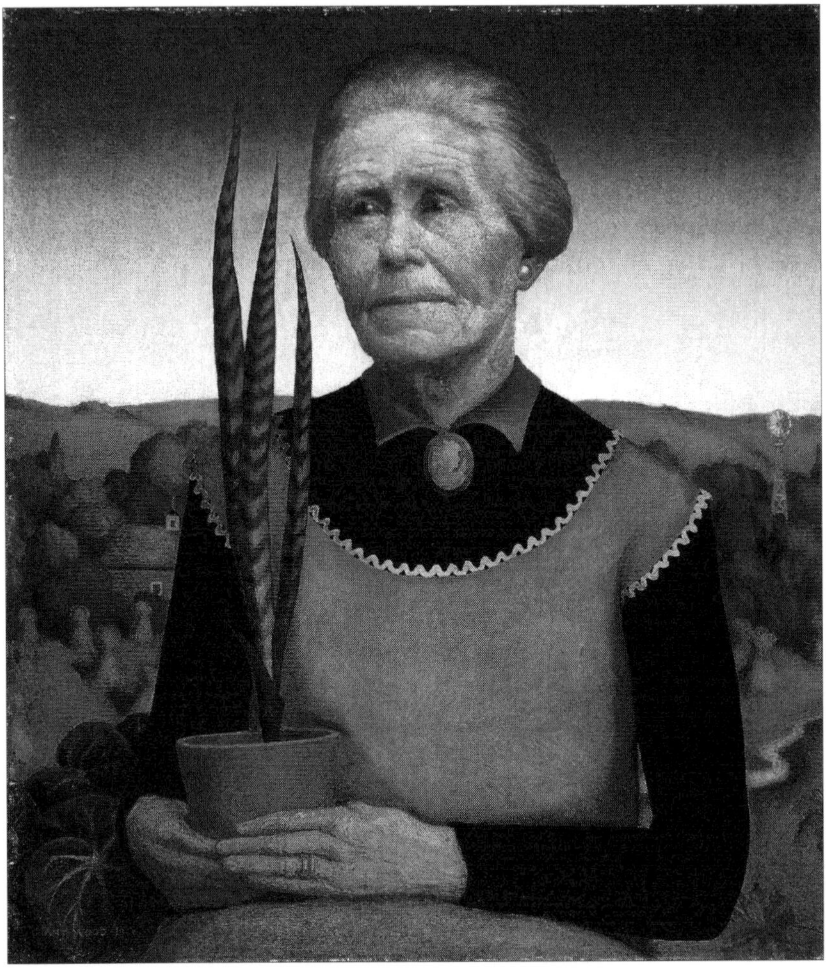

Grant Wood, Woman with Plants, 1929. Oil on upsom board, 20 ½ x 17 7/8 in. Cedar Rapids Museum of Art, Museum purchase. 31.1

porch having one of their lively discussions. Grant was extolling the beauties and excitements of Paris. 'Stuck-in-the-mud' Jay was countering with arguments about the beauties of Iowa, and suggested that Grant should quit running to France and stop being a French copycat. He argued that Grant should stay home and paint what he knew best, Iowa. Jay needled Grant until his dander rose. Up the street were

> two brightly colored quilts hanging on a clothesline. Jay called Grant's attention to the color and beauty of the scene. Grant painted *Quilts* [see page 21] in the summer of 1928. This painting was done in his impressionist style, but was the start of his using Iowa subjects in a style that was to make him famous."[61]

Their conversations must have been echoing in Grant Wood's head because, when the artist made his final trip to Europe in 1928, he was struck by the style of 16th century Flemish artists and found himself realizing that he could symbolize hard-working Iowans in much the same way. Grant began making use of, *"such commonplace things of American rural life as rickrack braid on dresses, wire fencing, overalls, and mechanically spaced cornfields."*[62] Upon his return from this 1928 trip he tried his first neo-Flemish painting: *Woman with Plants* (left). He used his mother as his model and posed her against a distinctively Midwestern landscape. He painted the image with glazes on composition board, in imitation of the old masters' techniques, stiffened her outlines, gave her face descriptive detail, and made her costume into simple decorative patterns, all lessons he had absorbed from the Flemish painters.

Woman with Plants looked, as one commentator put it, "rather like a Mona Lisa against an Iowa landscape."[63] And a review in Cedar Rapids praised *Woman with Plants* by saying, "Wood is now doing with pigments what Jay Sigmund is doing with words."[64] Grant Wood had reached a defining moment in his career.

The year 1928 became a turning point, not only for Grant Wood, but for the entire community. In March of that year, Cedar Rapids was awarded $50,000 by the Carnegie Foundation to participate in an experiment being run by the American Federation of Art. The foundation hoped to prove that, with an initial opportunity such as it provided, the community would become so thoroughly engrossed in the development and appreciation of its cultural influences they would become permanent values.[65]

Satisfied with its selection of a city—one which had industry and where the agricultural influence was strong— the Carnegie organization dispatched Edward B. Rowan to Cedar Rapids to serve as project director. Rowan's assignment was to exhibit and promote art appreciation by both bringing in traveling collections and encouraging local artists. Gallery space was opened in a smallish store room at 839 First Avenue SE, opposite the Montrose Hotel. Later, Mrs. Austin Palmer, who had inherited a fortune from her late husband's Palmer Penmanship Method, permitted the Rowans to convert her home beside the Ausadie apartments on First Avenue into space needed for the project: Cedar Rapids' Little Gallery opened in 1931 (313 Third St. SE.)[66]

From its earliest days, the Little Gallery offered many excellent traveling shows and became a popular showplace for all kinds of creative talent in the community. Cedar Rapids was suddenly being hailed throughout the state as a "real art center," and across the nation as the "prairie art capital."[67]

Paintings by local artists Grant Wood, Marvin Cone, and Adrian Dornbush were displayed in the earliest exhibitions. Books hand bound by Mrs. George Douglas and even a small sculpture by Grant's sister Nan were also on display. People from all walks of life were invited to receptions where typical entertainment might include the playing of compositions by

Louise Crawford of Coe College, and the reading of original manuscripts by Jay Sigmund.[68]

According to Mrs. C. Harve Geiger, whose husband was formerly dean of Coe College:

> "Through the ingenuity of both Mr. and Mrs. Rowan the Victorian (Palmer) house was transformed into a gallery, not only for the hanging of current shows of note, but there was a studio where children found self-expression through the medium of finger painting, crayons, metal work, and water colors; a workshop where embryo writers worked under Jay Sigmund, and Sadie Seagrave [from Oakdale] to produce poets...each paying a dime to help defray expenses of sandwiches and coffee. It was fun and inspirational."[69]

Show after show was brought to Cedar Rapids. All were successful. People flocked to the Little Gallery, discussed art over cups of tea beside the samovar at opening receptions, and had the privilege of meeting a number of America's foremost painters. The Little Gallery Writing Group, sponsored by Mr. Rowan, ran meetings over several years, most in the gallery itself, but some in the home of Mrs. Arthur Erskine.[70]

Over a six-year period, the Foundation spent $75,000 on the Little Gallery in Cedar Rapids. Both Wood and Cone, as well as Jay, benefited from the new community commitment to culture and, in return, they became catalysts for the developing artistic tradition of Cedar Rapids.[71]

In fact, one of the first students to enroll under Jay G. Sigmund's tutelage in the Little Gallery's writing program was a young Paul Engle.[72]

Born in 1908 and growing up as Jay's neighbor, Paul Engle was no stranger to his writing instructor.[73]

> "When I was a little boy living at the corner of 5th Avenue and 16th Street SE in Cedar Rapids, a quiet man, Jay G. Sigmund, perhaps a little heavy, with gentle voice and eyes as deep as farm wells, lived across the street. As I grew up, Jay was there as a living presence of poetry for me. I began to write poetry and when Jay discovered that curious fact he loaned me books, the first modern poems I had ever read. They were an astonishment and a revelation. Every young kid wanting to write should be so lucky. Thanks to him, on that typical street of Midwestern wooden houses, I entered a new world and have never left it, nor will I, until that door shuts finally."[74]

In the summer of 1932, just a year after the opening of the Little Gallery, Grant Wood, Ed Rowan, and gallery instructor Adrian Dornbush, took over some abandoned buildings in Stone City, Iowa, and established the Stone City Art Colony. Coe College offered course credit for students who, along with many of the instructors, came from all over the country.

> "I'm Bob Proost, a sign painter from Clinton, Iowa, a former commercial artist and a student at the Stone City Art Colony of 1932. That was the year I graduated from high school, and that's the spring, while I was a student at Mont St. Clare Academy of Clinton, that we were planning a picnic for the class. I grew up hearing of the beauty of Stone City and of its fine people, so I persuaded the class to have our picnic at Stone City. After spending the day there with the

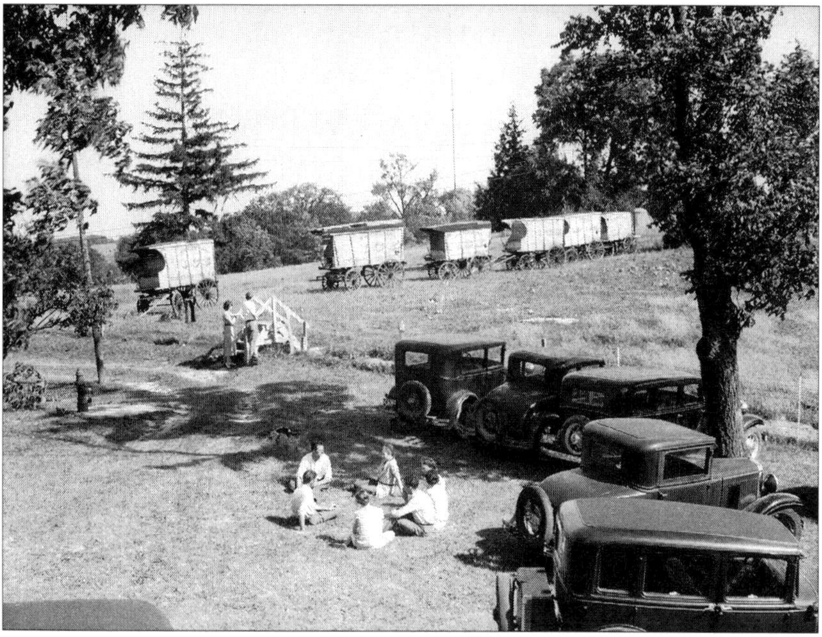

Stone City Art Colony photo, John W. Barry, Ice Wagons, Stone City, 1932-1933. Photograph, Cedar Rapids Museum of Art. 89.2.16

> class, I knew I had to come back that summer to see if I couldn't possibly put on canvas some of the beauty that Jay Sigmund poetically spoke of as he described the Wapsipinicon River carving its path through the stone hills we now love so much."[75]

At the height of the Depression, when few people had money to travel, the colony provided stimulus and excitement for the local community. People from across eastern Iowa turned out to visit the colony. On Sundays, as many as a thousand patrons paid the ten cent admission as well as bought sandwiches and soft drinks to help defray expenses. They gathered to hear Jay Sigmund read his poetry in the evening and, earlier in the day, act as emcee when musicians from the vicinity played the dulcimer, fiddle, or accordion. The ice house became an exhibition headquarters where works of art were sold to the visiting farmers and neighboring townspeople.[76]

I discovered an interesting story about traveling to Stone City. Originally pathways were carved out by pioneers as they crossed by wagon or by foot west as they crossed the Mississippi. Some were being paved to make way for modern transportation. One such ridge road, as they were called, ran between Waubeek and Stone City and acted as a main route to the art colony.

One day, toward the end of the 1933 season, as he was traveling there, Jay Sigmund had an unfortunate accident on Linn County's very own ridge road.[77] Sigmund's daughter-in-law, Virgina, describes the accident here:

> "My husband [Jim Sigmund] was driving. They were on their way to Stone City, to the Art Colony, where Jay was going to emcee the Sunday afternoon program. Father [Jay] was up front on the passenger side next to the window. As they came to a curve, a car came along on the wrong side and struck their car. Jay was taken to the hospital in Anamosa. The worst part was that he lost the ends of his fingers.[78]

As news of the accident spread, friends and family surrounded Jay Sigmund with love and expressions of concern including this note from Paul Engle:

> August 1933
> Dear Jay,
> I called your house after hearing of your accident Monday and Tuesday, and had to leave for Chicago without getting a response. So now I write to tell you how awfully sorry I am. I think I can realize a little better than most people what the loss of that finger with which one writes must mean, and I only

hope that you can keep your pecker up. As I feel you will. After all, writing is mostly done behind the eyes and I am certain you will be able to adapt yourself to the new life somehow. My sympathy also goes to Mrs. Sigmund. I don't know of any misfortune that has happened to anyone in Cedar Rapids that has elicited as much regret and real sincere good wishes as yours.—Paul[79]

Many of the Stone City artists sketched personal get-well cards. Of course, Grant Wood painted:

VIRGINIA: In his painting, Grant Wood made the car large and scary. The telephone poles looked like crosses in a cemetery. It's one of his only scary paintings. It showed how worried they were about Jay, but also about separating people from the soil and how there

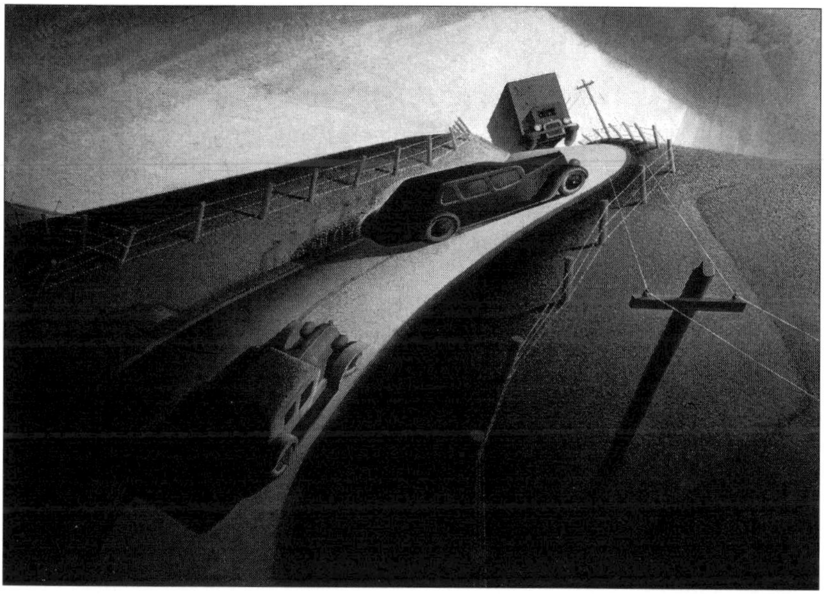

Grant Wood (American, 1892-1942), Death on the Ridge Road, 1935, oil on masonite, frame: 39 x 46 1/16 in. (99 x 117 cm), Williams College Museum of Art, Williamstown, MA, Gift of Cole Porter (47.1.3)

> were fewer horses due to modernization. It was a time of big transition.[80]

Wood's most sober assessment of modernity's impact on country living, *Death on the Ridge Road,* (above) was directly related to his friendship with Jay Sigmund. Three vehicles are traveling a steeply pitched and curving "ridge road." We don't know if the vehicles will crash, but we do know they are on a collision course, the artist's metaphor for the social upheavals of his own times.[81]

By this time, Grant Wood was one of a few being nationally acknowledged as leaders of Regionalist art. His work was associated with images of rolling Midwestern farmlands, industrious farm folk, and hand-guided walking plows cutting into rich loam. When he painted *Death on the Ridge Road,* it was pretty much of a surprise.

As it happened, however, the media were giving considerable attention to the increasing number and devastation of highway accidents at this time. By framing his narrative in terms of motor travel, and showing a dark side to technology, Wood was seen to demonstrate a critical edge and a machine-age mentality that appealed to urbanites. When *Death on the Ridge Road* was exhibited at his one-man show in New York City, it became a resounding success and generated headline-making-attendance figures along with complimentary reviews in *Newsweek, Time,* and *The New York Times.*[82]

Ironically Sigmund, who never drove a car, was known for his fear of technology:

> Sigmund fretted that increasing technology separated farmers from their horses and, in the final analysis,

> distanced them from the soil. His fear of urban growth and the accompanying decline of rural influence permeated many of his works...suggesting that the relentless march of modernization was threatening the entire existence of an earlier Iowa.[83]

Sigmund's poem, "Death Rides a Rubber Shod Horse," excerpted here, was probably written before the accident as he was concentrating more on short stories at the time. But this excerpt shows how strikingly similar his ideas were to those expressed in Grant Wood's painting:

> Death used to ride a white-maned horse
> Before these grey roads lined the sod.
> But now he travels on his course
> Astride a sleek thing, rubber-shod.[84]

Though financial problems eventually caused the Stone City Art colony to close after only two summers (1932-1933), the explicitly Regionalist venture had gone beyond the Midwest. Franklin Roosevelt named Ed Rowan Assistant Director to the Public Works of Art Project, the first of the New Deal's federally funded art efforts. Rowan and his family moved to Washington, DC. Sadly, the Little Gallery closed and the Art Association pictures were taken back to their permanent gallery in the Cedar Rapids Public Library.

Jay Sigmund, who had gained recognition for his poetry, was asked to write the introduction to the *Guide to Cedar Rapids and Northeast Iowa,* as part of the Federal Writers' Project guide series for each state.[85] [86]

Sigmund responded with a beautiful eight stanza narrative poem of the history of Cedar Rapids, excerpted here:

> Their hammer blows
> Came ringing down the morning, year on year:
> The Seasoned timber made their strong roof-trees
> And limestone from the river cliffs their hearths;
> Slowly, but with the sureness of the moon
> As it goes swinging through the night's dark arch,
> A city grew apace among these knolls—
> A clean white city by a silver stream.[87]

Grant Wood, by this time, had become an associate professor in the art department of The University of Iowa, at that time known as the State University of Iowa, and was appointed Iowa's Art Project Director for the WPA. In March of 1935, Grant married Sarah Sherman Maxon and the couple moved to a rented cottage in Waubeek that summer.[88]

Though not connected to the New Deal, but certainly connected, like Grant, to Jay Sigmund, Paul Engle also brought fame to Cedar Rapids. His ability as a poet, recognized when he graduated from Coe College, secured him an MA from the University of Iowa. His first book of poems, written as a thesis, earned him a fellowship to Columbia University. At Columbia, the young poet was awarded the prestigious Rhodes Scholarship which gave him three years of study at Oxford University in England.[89]

By 1934, Engle's book *American Song* had gained him world-wide recognition. This review from *The New York Times* is a perfect example:

> Rarely is a first book of poetry reviewed on the front page of this section or for that matter, any book of contemporary poetry, but Paul Engle's *American Song* has a natural title for that place. Both on the ground of its own distinguished quality and for its significance as an indicator of changing mood and temper among creative writers of the youngest generation, it merits the widest possible attention.[90]

Just like his mentor, Paul never lost sight of his roots. *American Song* included a dedication to "JGS":

> Vienna, July 31, 1934
> Dear Jay,
> This letter comes to you with knowledge it is overdue, but you must think of my half hazard, wandering existence here and forgive it.
> By now you will have had *American Song*, and found your own self in it. I hope you will accept the dedication of the earth section, as the one I feel is closest to you. It is the most actual way, perhaps the one most agreeable to you, by which I can define my friendship to you, and my gratitude for your constant helpfulness in the past, and above all, for your encouragement in those leanest, hardest years when my verse was turned down, evermore, rightly enough, G-d knows![91]
> — Paul

In that same month and year, July of 1934, after the highly successful showing of *Death on the Ridge Road* in New York and having recently completed *Dinner for Threshers*, a painting highly reminiscent of his boyhood, Wood decided a celebration was in

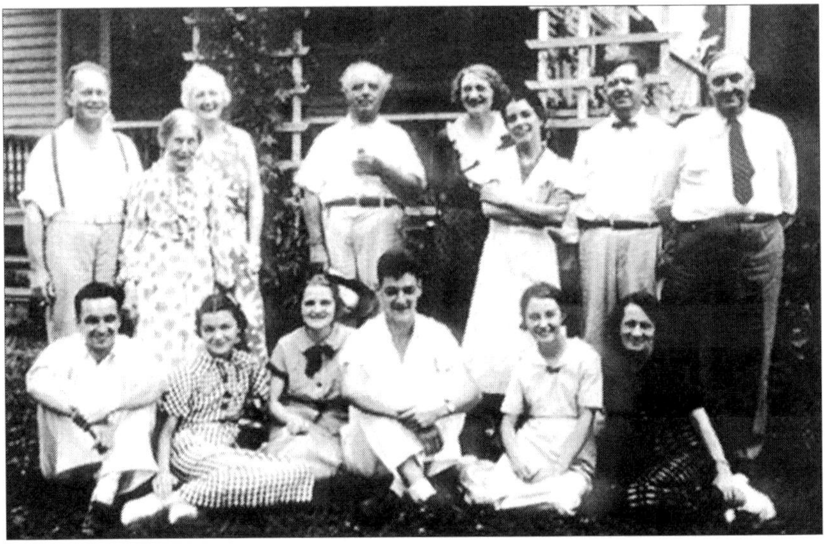

The Woods and Sigmunds with guests gathered for a dinner. Top: Grant, mother Hattie, wife Sarah, Charles Finger and family, Frank Luther Mott, Jay Sigmund. Bottom: Jim Sigmund, Mary Sigmund, Virginia Sigmund (later Meyers) unknown friend of family, Jane Sigmund (later Cooper) and Jay's wife, Louise.[93]

order. His wife Sarah and Jay Sigmund's wife Louise suggested they throw a dinner party. Invitations were sent out to friends who included Newbury Award winning author, Charles J. Finger and his family visiting from Arkansas, and Pulitzer Prize winning Professor of Journalism at the University of Iowa, Frank Luther Mott and his family.

> VIRGINIA: "Sarah used the Sigmunds' red checkered table cloth as it was the one in the *Dinner for Threshers* painting. The men at this dinner party, which was held in Waubeek, had a very heated discussion after dinner. Mrs. Wood and some of the other women were chuckling at them, but four months later, their conversations resulted in the publishing of *Revolt*

> *Against the City,* Wood's pamphlet-sized manifesto on Regionalism."[92]

Revolt Against the City, the first in the, "Whirling World Series" published in Iowa City by Frank Luther Mott, proved to be a turning point in helping to make Regionalism a nationally recognized movement.[94]

In it, Wood explained how the Great Depression had taught everyone many things, not the least of which was self-reliance:

> "It has thrown down the Tower of Babel erected in the years of a false prosperity; it has sent men and women back to the land; it has caused us to rediscover some of the old frontier virtues..."

He goes on to mention examples. Here he is referring to Paul Engle's recently published *American Song,* a book so popular that he doesn't even seem to see the need to include the title:

> "We still send scholars to Oxford, but it is significant that Paul Engle produces on his scholarship time one of the most American volumes of recent verse."[95]

Here Wood quotes Christopher Morley:

> "When Christopher Morley was out in Iowa last fall, he remarked on its freedom, permitting expansion with space and relaxing conditions for work. 'Future artists,' he observed, 'are more likely to come from the remoter areas, farther from the claims and distractions of an accelerating civilization.'

And, lastly, we read of Jay G. Sigmund:

> "My friend and fellow-townsman Jay Sigmund devotes his leisure hours to the writing of verses celebrating

Excerpt from Visitor

I knew he held the tang of stack and mow—
One sensed that he was brother to the soil;
His palms were stained with signs of stable toil
And calloused by the handles of his plough.

He told me how the creek had changed its bed,
And how his acres spread across the hill;
The hours wore and he was talking still
And I was hungry for the things he said.

Then I who long had pitied peasant folk
And broken faith with field and pasture ground
Felt dull and leaden-footed in my round
And strangely like a cart-beast with a yoke![98]

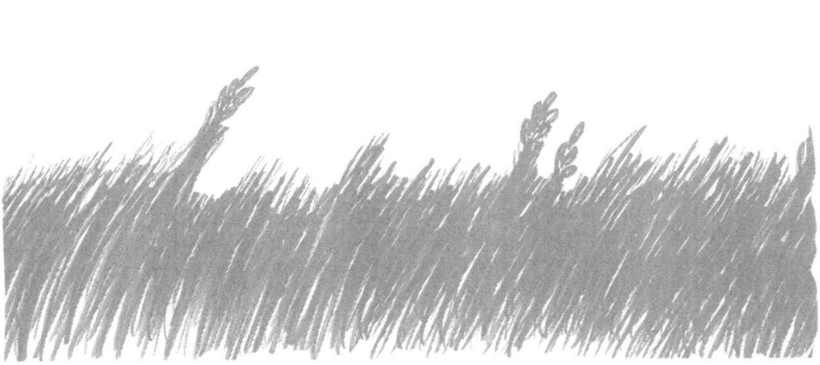

> the kind of human beings I have been discussing. I wish to quote his poem "Visitor" in this place.[96]

Christopher Morley let the nation know about his visit to Waubeek:

> "As a special Christmas pleasure, I print below a cut of Mr. Grant Wood's latest painting, *Dinner for Threshers*. I suppose in the enchanting village of Waubeek, where Jay Sigmund, poet and storyteller and insurance official, has preserved an old family cottage exactly as it was seventy years (Stuffed with Currier and Ives) I found relics which seemed queer so far inland. The village was first settled by sons of New England fishermen. On one house two anchors are carved on either side of a heart; in the blacksmith shop, Mr. Bruce, the smith, preserves an old harpoon. In his spare time, Mr. Bruce makes beautiful miniature hammers and other tools, each worthy to be a museum piece, and gives them away to lovers of good work."[97]

Seemingly never daunted by new writing challenges, Sigmund delved into the art of writing drama. With the guidance of Betty Smith, best known for her 1942 novel, *A Tree Grows in Brooklyn*, he published twenty-five one-act plays, five of which Smith co-authored. And, he even had a hand in writing the lyrics to some songs. Collaborating with Miss Louise Crawford, a professor in the department of music at Coe College, Sigmund wrote the lyrics to her 2 keys (high and low voice) in the dramatic song, "Fallen Oak" which was published by the White-Smith Music Publishing Company of Boston. The last verse of this song is:

Some demon must have forged the steel
Which chiseled through its hole:
G-d, what things must the chopper feel
Who kills a great oak's soul![99]

As might be expected, Sigmund began working on a first full length novel, *Purple Washboards*. Sadly, the novel was not to be. For, on October 19, 1937, Jay G. Sigmund died.

> "Mr. Sigmund was accidentally shot in the leg by a discharge from his own shotgun as he lost his footing while walking up a slight incline pursuing a rabbit he had wounded. The discharge almost tore his leg away, but he maintained consciousness and his shouts attracted help from a nearby house."[100]

As the news spread, friends and family shared in their grief:

> "Marvin Cone drove out to Stone City October 20, 1937, and told me of Jay Sigmund's death. It was a dark day, rain coming up in flurries. I was chopping wood. We stood and looked down at the Wapsie, flowing with an autumn brown. I had been walking along it the day before, at the same hour when Jay was lying in the field calling for help in the empty air.... We put the wood on the fire, and sat there, but talking was no good."[101]—Paul Engle

> "I cried terribly when I fully understood that he was gone. He was such a good man...I know that I have lost one of the finest friends I've ever had...His sweet and warm attitude towards life and towards people convinced me of something I had never believed before: That there are good and decent people in the world. And he was one of the best of these. I cannot say any more than this."[102]—Betty Smith

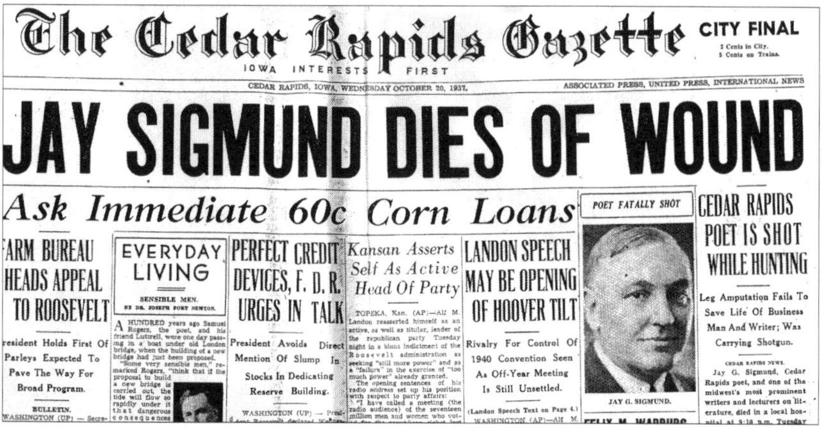

The Cedar Rapids Gazette

CITY FINAL

3 Cents in City. 5 Cents on Trains.

IOWA INTERESTS FIRST

CEDAR RAPIDS, IOWA, WEDNESDAY OCTOBER 20, 1937.

ASSOCIATED PRESS, UNITED PRESS, INTERNATIONAL NEWS

JAY SIGMUND DIES OF WOUND

Ask Immediate 60c Corn Loans

FARM BUREAU HEADS APPEAL TO ROOSEVELT

President Holds First Of Parleys Expected To Pave The Way For Broad Program.

BULLETIN.

WASHINGTON (UP) — Secre-

EVERYDAY LIVING

SENSIBLE MEN.

BY DR. JOSEPH FORT NEWTON.

A HUNDRED years ago Samuel Rogers, the poet, and his friend Luttrell, were one day passing in a boat under old London bridge, when the building of a new bridge had just been proposed.

"Some very sensible men," remarked Rogers, "think that if the proposal to build a new bridge is carried out, the tide will flow so rapidly under it that dangerous consequences

PERFECT CREDIT DEVICES, F. D. R. URGES IN TALK

President Avoids Direct Mention Of Slump In Stocks In Dedicating Reserve Building.

WASHINGTON (UP) — President Roosevelt declared Wednes-

Kansan Asserts Self As Active Head Of Party

TOPEKA, Kan. (AP)—Alf M. Landon reasserted himself as an active, as well as titular, leader of the republican party Tuesday night in a blunt indictment of the Roosevelt administration as seeking "still more power" and as a "failure" in the exercise of "too much power" already granted.

The opening sentences of his radio address set up his position with respect to party affairs:

"I have called a meeting (the radio audience) of the seventeen million men and women who vot-

LANDON SPEECH MAY BE OPENING OF HOOVER TILT

Rivalry For Control Of 1940 Convention Seen As Off-Year Meeting Is Still Unsettled.

(Landon Speech Text on Page 4.)

WASHINGTON (AP)—Alf M.

POET FATALLY SHOT

JAY G. SIGMUND.

FELIX M. WARBURG

CEDAR RAPIDS POET IS SHOT WHILE HUNTING

Leg Amputation Fails To Save Life Of Business Man And Writer; Was Carrying Shotgun.

CEDAR RAPIDS NEWS.

Jay G. Sigmund, Cedar Rapids poet, and one of the midwest's most prominent writers and lecturers on literature, died in a local hospital at 9:10 p.m. Tuesday

Front page of the *Cedar Rapids Gazette* announcing Jay Sigmund's death.

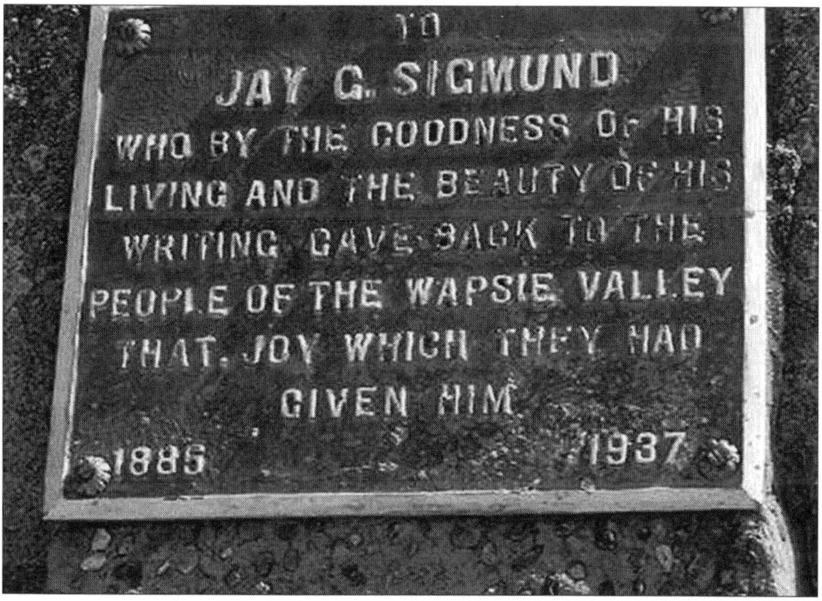

Front of Jay Sigmund's memorial stone beside the old store in Waubeek, currently FB&Co.

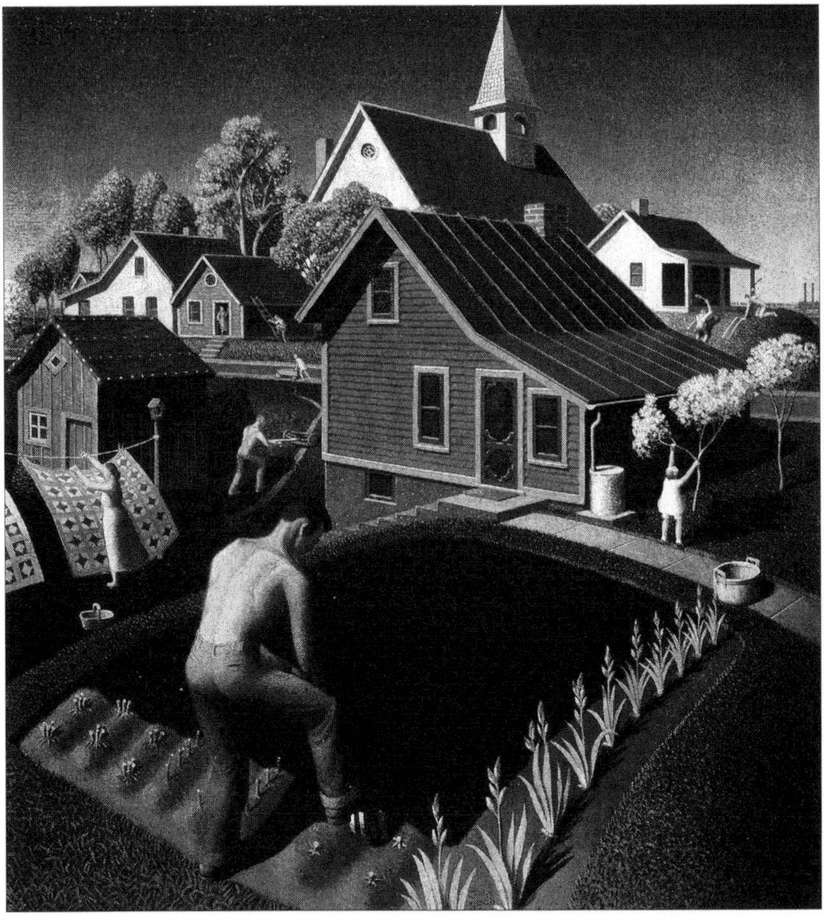

Grant Wood, *Spring in Town*, 1941, oil on Masonite panel, Collection of the Swope Art Museum, Terre Haute, Indiana; 1941.30;

> "Jay Sigmund is not dead. 'He has not gone, only in the flesh—the lovely spirit of his poetry will inspire us. I shall go through the remaining days of my life thanking G-d I knew him and envious of those who knew him better."[103]—Father Campbell

Beside the old stone store in Waubeek, a memorial stone was placed by Jay Sigmund's friends with a bronze tablet. Unveiled by two-year-old grandson Jay G. Sigmund II, son of James and Virginia.

Grant Wood, too upset to attend the funeral or memorials, made his statement in his final painting, completed in 1941. *Spring in Town* (previous page), clearly depicted its theme: Spring heralds the folk's renewal of their cycle with the earth and everyone is included.[104] The lines of the house, the preparation of the garden, the church steeple across the road, and the colorful quilts airing on the clothesline, were painted in Iowa City, but surely, as Jay's young grandson exclaimed upon seeing it, "That's Papa's house!"[105]

The Sigmund family and I truly believe this painting by Wood represented the Waubeek cabin that served as a retreat to Jay G. Sigmund who, in his own way, helped inspire Midwest Regionalism.

> "It is not chance that the amount of writing and painting of high order in the Waubeek-Cedar Rapids region has been so great. It is not chance that Grant Wood and Marvin Cone should paint where Jay Sigmund has written and where from the beginning he could give them hearty encouragement and full wisdom. The powerful impulse to utter not only the private life of the artist but the public life of a district, has spread outward from the valley of the Wapsipinicon to the valley of the Cedar and now, at the state university, to the valley of the Iowa. Like the most ancient cultures and commerce, it has followed the rivers...Here again is a thing not of Cedar Rapids, but of America."[106]

Several generations have passed since the days Jay Sigmund roamed the woods and river banks along the Wapsipinicon River. And it's well over a decade since I began my journey to understand him. In that time, daughter-in-law, Virginia Sigmund Myers, died at age ninety-three and Jay Sigmund's daughter, Jane Elizabeth Cooper, died as I was finishing up the second take on the manuscript for this book. She was ninety-nine. I felt a deep loss with the passing of these two classy ladies, my last personal connections to the Jay Sigmund story.

I need not worry about his legacy though. These examples comfort me.

On December 31, 2017 and January 7, 2018, *The Cedar Rapids Gazette* carried two articles by Linn-Mar teacher John Lawrence Hanson. The first, "Enjoying the Silence of Nature," is illustrated with a close-up of the rock, plaque, and site of the Jay G. Sigmund Memorial Park in Waubeek. "A Cold, quiet morning along the Wapsi," the second of the two-part series, is illustrated with tunnels of field mice on a cold morning along the Wapsipinicon River and includes two excerpts of Jay Sigmund's poetry.

The following words by Pulitzer–prize-winning art critic, Philip Kennicott, appeared in the *Washington Post* on March 2, 2018. When describing "American Gothic and Other Fables," an exhibit being held at New York City's Whitney, Mr. Kennicott wrote:

> "Like Thorton Wilder's *Our Town* and Aaron Copland's *Appalachian Spring,* Wood's *American Gothic* both defines and defies Americana, establishing a sense of American identity."

A later quote from the article referred to *Death on the Ridge Road*:

> "One painting, made in 1935, stands out among the others for its symbolic power. In it, we discover

> the coexistence of different forces and potentials as unresolved in their intersections as our sense of both the past and future."

Lastly, "Visitors arrive to engage in Iowa Traditions," an article in the April 5, 2018 edition of the *Cedar Rapids Gazette,* describes how Iowa City is really vibrant as it plays host to two things for which the community is recognized around the world: writing and wrestling.

> "The writing segment refers to Iowa City being chosen as host to the annual meeting of UNESCO's Cities of Literature because Iowa City is celebrating its 10th anniversary of that designation. Representatives of literature were expected to attend from twenty-eight different countries."

My research on how Iowa City earned this honor takes us back to Paul Engle, long time director of the University of Iowa's Writing Workshop and founder, with wife, Hualing, of the university's International Writing Workshop.

These recent articles give me the security of knowing Jay Sigmund's influence flourishes to this day. Perhaps you will even permit me to say almost all things cultural in Iowa began somewhere along the Road to Waubeek.

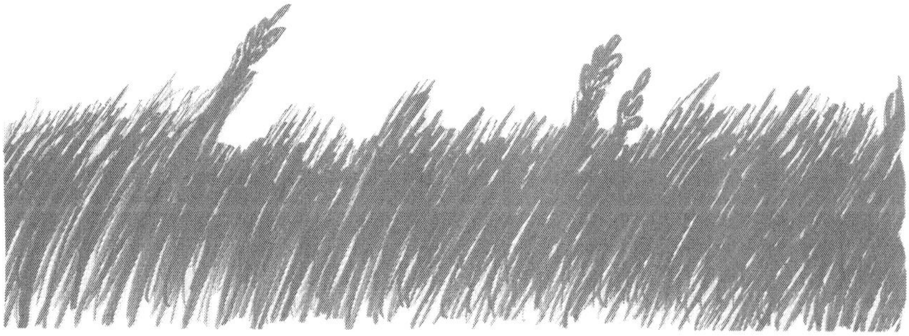

Acknowledgements:

I wish to thank Mr. Sigmund's grandchildren, Jan and Cheri Dickey and Larry Cooper, as well as historian Mark Stoffer Hunter for their help. I could not have done this without you! I would also like to acknowledge Gerald Lowenberg, Chris Lynch, Heidi Berger, and Ray and Steve Feller for their continued encouragement in this project. Ultimately, I thank Steve Semken for sharing my recognition of the importance of the story of Jay G. Sigmund.

Notes:

1. Carnegie Aid Gave C.R. Big Boost in Art, John Reynolds, *The Cedar Rapids Gazette,* Sunday, August 11, 1946, p.6B.

2. Sherman, William, Editor, *Iowa's Country Schools: Landmarks in Learning,* Mid-Prairie Books, Parkersburg, Iowa, 1998.

3. Sigmund, Jay G., Letter to Dr. C.G. Stookey, Carl and Mary Koehler History Center Archives, November 14, 1933.

4. Sherman, William L., *Iowa's Country Schools: Landmarks of Learning,* Iowa State Education Association and Mid Prairie Books, Ames, Iowa, 1998.

5. I was to come across several descriptions of the story of Grant Wood's painting The Quilts. I believe the words of Edward Ferreter's *Grant Wood Meets Jay Sigmund,* as seen here, say it best.

6. Mott, Frank Luther, The Society of Prevention of Cruelty to Speakers, *The Palimpsest,* State Historical Society of Iowa, Vol. XLIII, no. 3, March 1962, pgs. 117–118.

7. Mott, Frank Luther, The Society of Prevention of Cruelty to Speakers, *The Palimpsest,* State Historical Society of Iowa, Vol. XLIII, No. 3, March 1962, pgs. 113–128, cover, and center insert pages of photographs between pgs. 128 & 129.

8. Smith, Roland http://www.press-citizen-media.com/150/smith.html

9. Engle, Paul, *A Lucky American Childhood,* University of Iowa Press, Iowa City, 1996, pgs. 64–65.

10. Milosch, Jane, C., *Grant Wood's Studio: Birthplace of American Gothic, A Decorative Adventure,* Prestel Press, Munich, Germany, for the Cedar Rapids Museum of Art, 2005, pg. 98.

11. Brown, Hazel, *Grant Wood and Marvin Cone: Artists of an Era,* Iowa State University Press, Ames, Iowa, 1972, pgs. 67–68.

12. Myers, Virginia Sigmund, "Esther and Robert Armstrong Plan their New Home: Pleasant Hill, a description written for me on March 18, 2005.

13. Interview in an Announcement of Distinction, *Cedar Rapids Republican,* November, 1924.

14. IBID

15. Special Collections Papers of Jay G. Sigmund, University of Iowa Library.

16. https://en.wikipedia.org/wiki/Order_of_Owls, last edited July 2016.

17. *A History of Central City and the Surrounding Area, 1839–1989,* compiled by The Central City Historical Society, co-editors Mary Shakespeare Somers and Belvan Butters Abernathy, Fourth Street Publishing, Central City, Iowa.

18. Jack, Zachary Michael, *The Plowman Sings: The Essential Fiction, Poetry, and Drama of America's Forgotten Regionalist Jay G. Sigmund,* University Press of America, Lanham Maryland, 2008.

19. Ferreter, Ed, *Jay Sigmund's Wapsipinicon Valley,* University of Iowa, 1987.

20. A permanent collection of his work is now housed at the Dubuque Museum of Art. For more information, check: www.encyclopediadubuque.org/Glassell.

21. Interview at Marion, Iowa, home of Jane Cooper, August, 2015.

22. Cheri was referring to Granger House, an historic house museum in Marion, Iowa, where we worked together after my years at the History Center.

23. August 11, 2015 taped interview with daughter Jane Cooper.

24. https://en.wikipedia.org/wiki/Ovenbird:The ovenbird (Seiurus aurocapilla) is a small songbird of the New World warbler family (Parulidae). This migratory bird breeds in eastern North America and winters in Central America, many Caribbean Islands, Florida, and northern Venezuela.

25. Sigmund notes that frequent reference to "Fatal Wawbeek" or "Black Rock" is made in Longfellow's poem, "Hiawatha," when he wrote his own poem entitled "Waubeek."

26. Ferreter, Ed, *Introductory note to Sigmund's Wapsipinicon Valley,* University of Iowa, 1987.

27. Sigmund, Jay G., as printed in Jay Sigmund's *Wapsipinicon Valley,* University of Iowa, Iowa City, Iowa, July 26, 1987. Original date of poem is unknown.

28. Donated by his son, Jim, parts of Sigmund's collection was on display at the Carl and Mary Koehler History Center in Cedar Rapids, Iowa.

29. Heck, Susanne, *Encyclopedia of North American Indians, Fox/Mesquaki*, published on line through Central Missouri State University: http://college.hmco.com/history/readerscomp/naind/html/na-012600-foxmesquakie.htm.

30. Burns, E. Bradford, *Kinship with the Land: Regionalist Thought in Iowa*, University of Iowa Press, 1996, pgs. 46–47.

31. August 6, 2015 interview with daughter Jane Cooper and her son Larry: "He would speak at family reunions, the Art Colony, with boy scouts, 4H, and others."

32. "Arrowhead" appeared in Sigmund's first book of poetry, *Frescoes*, published by the B. J. Brimmer Company, Boston, 1922. These segments can be found on pgs 10–11.

33. Sigmund, Jay G., introduction to *The Wapsipinicon*, found in Papers of Jay G. Sigmund, Special Collections, and University of Iowa Library.

34. Jay Sigmund's *Wapsipinicon Valley*, edited by Ed Ferreter, University of Iowa International Writing Program 1987, pg.3.

35. Jay Sigmund's *Wapsipinicon Valley*, edited by Ed Ferreter, University of Iowa International Writing Program 1987, pg. 30.

36. Mott, Frank Luther, "The Midland," *The Palimpsest*, Volume XLIII, #3, State Historical Society of Iowa, Iowa City, March, 1962.

37. *Jay Sigmund's Wapsipinicon Velley*, edited by Ed Ferreter, University of Iowa International Writing program, 1987, pgs. 3.

38. "Drunken Land Owner," is from *Drowsy Ones*, Prairie Publishing Company, Cedar Rapids, Iowa, 1925, page 19.

39. "Central City Claims Real Poet," *Central City News*, (who included some quoting from the *Cedar Rapids Republican*), Thursday, November 9, 1922, Vo. XVI.

40. A flyer from James T. White & Company, 70 Fifth Avenue, New York, advertising Jay Sigmund's new book, *Pinions*, which was to appear on September 1, 1923.

41. Milton M. Reigelman, *The Midland: A Venture in Literary Regionalism*, U of I Press, Iowa City, 1975.

42. "Bankrupt Farmer's Auction" is from *Pinions*, James T. White and Company, New York, 1923, page 67.

43. Mott, Frank Luther, "The Midland," *The Palimpsest*, State Historical Society of Iowa, Iowa City Iowa, Volume XLIII, No. 3, March 1962.

44. Sigmund, Jay G., (First written and chosen as a selection for *The Midland* in 1924, "Retired," came out in *Drowsy Ones*, published by Prairie Publishing Company in Cedar Rapids, Iowa, 1925, pgs 9–10.

45. Milton M. Reigelman, *The Midland: A Venture in Literary Regionalism*, U of I Press, Iowa City, 1975.

46. Sigmund, Jay G., "The Bankrupt Farmer's Auction," *Pinions*, James T. White and Company, New York, 1923, pg. 67.

47. Sigmund, Jay G., First written and chosen as a s selection for *The Midland* in 1924, "Retired" came out in *Drowsy Ones*, published by Prairie Publishing Company in Cedar Rapids, Iowa 1925, pages 9–10.

48. Sigmund, Jay G., First written and chosen as a s selection for *The Midland* in 1924, "Retired" came out in *Drowsy Ones*, published by Prairie Publishing Company in Cedar Rapids, Iowa 1925, pages 9–10.

49. Carlson, Allan C. "Bard of the Wapsipinicon: An Assessment of Jay G. Sigmund," *Modern Age*, Vol. 55 #4, Fall 2013.

50. Sigmund, Jay G, Table of Contents, *Drowsy Ones*, Prairie Publishing Company, Cedar Rapids, Iowa, 1925.

51. Jeffers to Sigmund, letter in Special Collection Papers, Box 1, University of Iowa Library, June 22, 1926.

52. Mumford to Sigmund, letter in Special Collection Papers Box 1, File 2, December, 1931.

53. Anonymous (possibly Paul Engle, who was a student at Washington High School at this time), Interview with Mr. Sigmund, *The Pulse*, Volume XXV, #3, February, 1925, frontispiece and page 1.

54. Editors notes as found on flyleaf of *Wapsipinicon Tales*, The Prairie Publishing Company, Cedar Rapids, 1927.

55. Engle, Paul, "The Poet and the Man," introductory remarks in *Sigmund: Select Poetry and Prose*, written in Iowa City, November 8, 1939. This memorial book was published by Prairie Press in Muscatine.

56. E. Bradford Burns, *Kinship with the Land: Regionalist Thought in Iowa, 1894-1942*, University of Iowa Press, Iowa City, 1996, pg. 46.

57. Cedar Rapids Public Library Reference Paper # 89.316, Cedar Rapids Authors: Mr. Jay Sigmund, 1930.

58. E. Bradford Burns, *Kinship with the Land: Regionalist Thought in Iowa, 1894-1942*, University of Iowa Press, Iowa City, 1996, pgs.150–151.

59. Ed Ferreter's Master of Arts thesis "From Word to Image: Grant Wood Meets Jay G. Sigmund," published by the University of Iowa in 1985..

60. Ferreter, Edward Pierce, *From Word to Image: Grant Wood Meets Jay G. Sigmund*, University of Iowa Master's Thesis, 1985.

61. Quote of Grant Wood as found in *The Guide to Cedar Rapids and Northeast Iowa*, The Federal Writers' Works Progress Administration, State of Iowa, 1937, pages 24-25.

62. "Iowa's Art the Vogue," *Kansas City Star*, in Wood scrapbooks, AAA1216/301.

63. Corn, Wanda M., *Grant Wood: The Regionalist Vision*, Yale University Press, 1983. p. 33.

64. Murray, Janette Stevenson and Fredrick Gray, *The Story of Cedar Rapids*, New York, Stratford House, 1950, pgs. 212–215.

65. Corn, Wanda, *Grant Wood: The Regionalist Vision*, Yale University Press, New Haven, 1983.

66. Brown, Hazel, "The Little Gallery," *Grant Wood and Marvin Cone: Artists of an Era*, Iowa State University Press, Ames, Iowa, 1972, pgs. 70–74.

67. Corn, Wanda, *Grant Wood: The Regionalist Vision*, Yale University Press, New Haven, 1983.

68. Brown, Hazel, "The Little Gallery," *Grant Wood and Marvin Cone: Artists of an Era*, Iowa State University Press, Ames, Iowa, 1972, pgs. 70–74.

69. Clements, Ralph, *Tales of the Town: Little known anecdotes of life in Cedar Rapids*, Stamats Publishing Company, Cedar Rapids, 1967.

70. In 1962 the Rockefeller foundation supplied Mr. Engle with a $10,000 grant to seek out talented writers and encourage them to the Writers' Workshop at the University of Iowa. In his 1967 set of anecdotes, *Tales of the Town*, Ralph Clements states that according to one biographer, this unorthodox idea probably made the University of Iowa the best-known center for the teaching of creative writing in the United States.

71. Murray, Janette Stevenson and Fredrick Gray, *The Story of Cedar Rapids*, New York, Stratford House, 1950, pg.202.

72. Engle, Paul, *A Lucky American Childhood*, University of Iowa Press, 1996.

73. Paul Engle's essay "Jay G. Sigmund as Neighbor," *From Word to Image: Grant Wood Meets Jay G. Sigmund* a master's thesis by Edward Pierce Ferreter, 1985.

74. Quote from transcript of an audio tape done of Bob Proost by Irwin Lowe of Stone City, date unknown but probably about 1975.

75. Murray, Janette Stevenson and Fredrick Gray, *The Story of Cedar Rapids*, Stratford House, New York, 1950, pgs. 216–217.

76. Corn, Wanda, *Grant Wood: The Regionalist Vision*, Yale University Press, New Haven, 1983, pgs. 81–82.

77. Virginia Sigmund Myers, in August 2005 interview held at the Central City home of Sigmund's daughter Jane Cooper.

78. Excerpt of letter from Paul Engle to Jay Sigmund found in Papers of Paul Engle in archives of Stewart Memorial Library at Coe College.

79. Virginia Sigmund Myers in August 2005 interview held at the Central City home of Sigmund's daughter Jane Cooper.

80. Corn, Wanda, *Grant Wood: The Regionalist Vision*, Yale University Press, New Haven, 1983, pg. 82.

81. "Son of the Soul Masters Pointing before Showing in N.Y." *Newsweek*, April 20, 1935, "Wood Works" *Time*, April 23, 1935 and Grant Wood, Iowa Artist," *The New York Times*, April 21, 1930.

82. E. Bradford Burns, *Kinship with the Land*, University of Iowa Press, Iowa City, 1996, pg. 46.

83. Ferreter, Edward Pierce, *From Word to Image: Grant Wood Meets Jay G. Sigmund*, University of Iowa Press, 1985.

84. Reynolds, John, "Carnegie Aid Gave C.R. Big Boost in Art," *The Cedar Rapids Gazette*, Sunday, August 11, 1946, p.6B.

85. Corn, Wanda, *Grant Wood: The Regionalist Vision*, Yale University Press, New Haven, 1983

86. Sigmund, Jay G., "Cedar Rapids: A Poem," *Guide to Cedar Rapids and Northeast Iowa*, Laurence Press, Cedar Rapids, Iowa, 1937.

87. Meyers, Virginia Sigmund, Interview with Sigmund family, August 2005.

88. Murray, Janette Stevenson and Fredrick Gray, *The Story of Cedar Rapids*, Stratford House, New York, 1950, pgs. 216 -17,

89. *The New York Times Book Review*, July 29 1934.

90. Engle, Paul, July 31, 1934, excerpt of letter to Jay Sigmund from Vienna, Austria, Stewart Memorial Library Special Collections, Coe College, Cedar Rapids, Iowa.

91. Quotes of daughter-in-law, Virginia Sigmund Meyer, from August 2005 interview of Sigmund family in Central City, Iowa.

92. Virginia Sigmund Myers shared with me saying this is very rare, as both Grant Wood's mother and wife are in the photo.

93. Quotes of daughter-in-law, Virginia Sigmund Meyer, from August 2005 interview of Sigmund family in Central City, Iowa.

94. Wood is referring to one of Paul Engle's most enduring works, *American Song*. The book is dedicated, in part, to JGS, who is, of course Jay Sigmund. He is also referring to the Theater Arts Project for which Betty Smith is working with Sigmund.

95. Wood, Grant, *Revolt Against the City*, Whirling Word Series, Iowa City, 1935. Here it is excerpted.

96. Sigmund, Jay G., originally published in *Drowsy Ones*, Prairie Publishing Company, Cedar Rapids, 1925, pg. 17.

97. Morley, Christopher, editor, *The Saturday Review of Literature*, The Bowling Green, December 22, 1934, pg. 387.

98. Cedar Rapids Public Library Reference Paper # 89.316, Cedar Rapid Authors: Mr. Jay Sigmund~1930. (Original sheet music can be found in Stewart Memorial Library Archives, Coe College, Cedar Rapids, Ia.)

99. "Jay Sigmund Dies of Wound, Cedar Rapids Poet is Shot While Hunting," *The Cedar Rapids Gazette*, Wednesday, October 20, 1937, pg. 1.

100. Engle, Paul, Note, introductory remarks in *Sigmund: Select Poetry and Prose*, Prairie Press, Muscatine, Iowa, 1939.

101. A letter to J. Sigmund dated October 26th, 1937, from author Betty Smith, best known for her book *A Tree Grows in Brooklyn*. Original in University of Iowa Libraries, special collections, papers of Jay G. Sigmund, Iowa City, Iowa.

102. Father Campbell Speaking at Funeral Service, Extols Sigmund's Life and Writing, *The Cedar Rapids Gazette*, October 22, 1937, p.1. (The poetical quotation was taken from the final stanza of Sigmund's poem, "Stations of the Cross.")

103. E. Bradford Burns, *Kinship with the Land: Regionalist Thought in Iowa, 1894-1942*, University of Iowa Press, Iowa City, 1996, pg.174.

104. As told to the author by Sigmund's daughter-in-law, Virginia Sigmund Meyers.

105. Engle, Paul, introductory remarks in *Sigmund: Select Poetry and Prose*, Prairie Press, Muscatine, Iowa, November 8, 1939.

106. Ferreter, Ed, *Jay Sigmund's Wapsipinicon Valley*, University of Iowa, Iowa City, 1987, pg. 28.

Photo by Chris Lynch

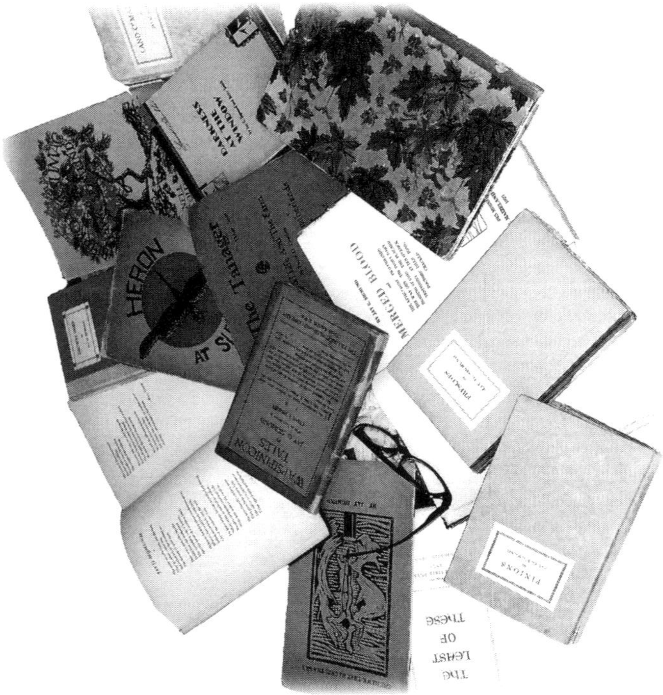

Works by Jay G. Sigmund

Books of Poetry and Prose:

Frescoes, (B.J. Brimmer Company, 1922)

Pinions, (James T. White & Company, 1923)

Land O'Maize Folk, (James T. White & Company, 1924)

Drowsy Ones, (Prairie Publishing Company 1925)

Wapsipinicon Tales, (Prairie Publishing Company, 1927)

Merged Blood and Other Stories, (Maizeland Press, 1929)

The Ridge Road, (Prairie Publishing Company, 1930)

The Least of These, (Prairie Press, 1935)

Select Poetry and Prose, (Edited by Paul Engle as a joint work with Ed Lowe, Marvin Cone, and Fred Poyneer, Prairie Press, Muscatine 1939)

Chapbooks:

Burr Oak & Sumac, (Cornell College, Mt. Vernon, Ia, 1936)

The Hawk that Haunts the Sky, (Coe College, 1937)

Heron at Sunset, (Cornell College, Mt. Vernon, Ia, 1938)

Plays:

Vine Leaves, (with Betty Smith, Samuel French, Circa 1936)

Folk Stuff, (with Betty Smith, Samuel French, New York, 1937)

Darkness at the Window, (with Betty Smith, Dramatic Publishing Company, Chicago, 1938)

Credits: All photos, unless noted, are provided by Barbara Feller and Virginia Sigmund Meyers collection.

Grant Wood, *Spring in Town,* 1941, oil on Masonite panel, Collection of the Swope Art Museum, Terre Haute, Indiana; 1941.30;

Grant Wood (American, 1892-1942) *Death on the Ridge Road,* 1935, oil on masonite frame: 39 x 46 1/16 in. (99 x 117 cm) Williams College Museum of Art, Williamstown, MA, Gift of Cole Porter (47.1.3).

Grant Wood, Woman with Plants, 1929. Oil on upsom board, 20 ½ x 17 7/8 in. Cedar Rapids Museum of Art, Museum purchase. 31.1

Stone City Art Colony photo, John W. Barry, Ice Wagons, Stone City, 1932-1933. Photograph, Cedar Rapids Museum of Art. 89.2.16

Grant Wood, Woman with Plants, 1929. Oil on upsom board, 20 ½ x 17 7/8 in. Cedar Rapids Museum of Art, Museum purchase. 31.1

Use of photo with Chrstopher Morley, Grant Wood, and Jay Sigmund courtesy of the Family of Jay G. Sigmund.

Paul Engle photo on page 26 courtesy of Stewart Memorial Library, Coe College

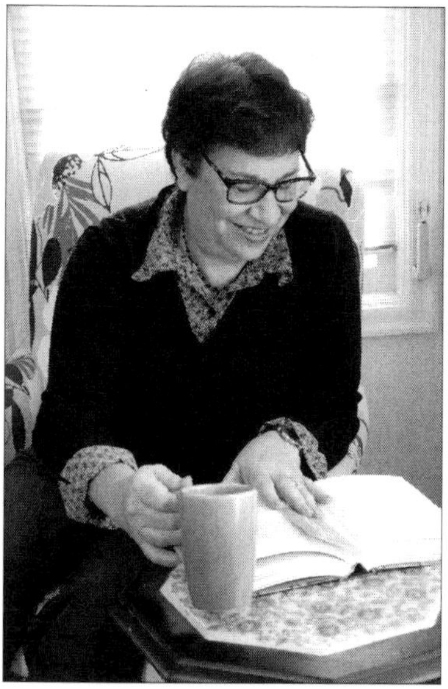

Native New Yorker, **Barbara Feller,** fell in love with Iowa and Iowans while working as an educator in area schools and museums. A part time teacher at Temple Judah since 1979, Barbara retired from her more public venue in 2013 with a desire to share inspiring stories of the history of her adopted community. Jay Sigmund and Grant Wood top that list.

When not teaching or writing, Barbara tries to keep up with husband Steve, daughters Heidi and Ray, sons-in-law Howard and Michael and four incredible grandchildren: Max, Isaac, Leo, and Ramona. She has traveled extensively with them, and enjoys gardening, reading, and cooking in her quieter moments.

Barbara is a member of the Wednesday Shakespeare Club, The Ladies' Literary Club of Cedar Rapids, Martha Marquis Book Club of Coe College, and SCBWI (The Society of Children's Book Authors and Illustrators).

Road to Waubeek is Barbara's first book, but there are plans for more.

The Ice Cube Press began publishing in 1991 to focus on how to live with the natural world and to better understand how people can best live together in the communities they share and inhabit. Using the literary arts to explore life and experiences in the heartland of the United States we have been recognized by a number of well-known writers including: Gary Snyder, Gene Logsdon, Wes Jackson, Patricia Hampl, Greg Brown, Jim Harrison, Annie Dillard, Ken Burns, Roz Chast, Jane Hamilton, Daniel Menaker, Kathleen Norris, Janisse Ray, Craig Lesley, Alison Deming, Harriet Lerner, Richard Lynn Stegner, Rhodes, Michael Pollan, David Abram, David Orr, and Barry Lopez. We've published a number of well-known authors including: Mary Swander, Jim Heynen, Mary Pipher, Bill Holm, Connie Mutel, John T. Price, Carol Bly, Marvin Bell, Debra Marquart, Ted Kooser, Stephanie Mills, Bill McKibben, Craig Lesley, Elizabeth McCracken, Derrick Jensen, Dean Bakopoulos, Rick Bass, Linda Hogan, Pam Houston, and Paul Gruchow. Check out Ice Cube Press books on our web site, join our email list, facebook group, or follow us on twitter. Visit booksellers, museum shops, or any place you can find good books and support true honest to goodness independent publishing projects so you can discover why we continue striving to "hear the other side."

Ice Cube Press, LLC (est. 1993)
North Liberty, Iowa, Midwest, USA
steve@icecubepress.com
twitter @icecubepress
www.icecubepress.com

to Fenna Marie and
the roads you'll travel—
some so curious and new,
others twisty weird and unexplored
a few well tried and true.